Edward Gerrard & Sons

A Taxidermy Memoir

by
P. A. Morris

Edward Gerrard & Sons- a taxidermy memoir.
First published in 2004
M. P. M.
West Mains, London Road
Ascot, Berkshire SL 5 7DG UK

ISBN 0 - 9545596 -1- 4

Text copyright © P. A. Morris, 2004

Printed by the Lavenham Press
Lavenham, Suffolk CO10 9RN

Acknowledgments

I thank the many people who have contributed material for this book. I am particularly grateful to Joan Gillett (manageress of Gerrard Hire Ltd), who so often entertained me with tales of old, in between trying to answer telephone calls in her tiny office. She also kindly allowed me the run of the hire stock, among which I enjoyed discovering so many extraordinary artefacts. John & Betty Holdcroft and Audrey Durambeys were most helpful in providing details of their family and kindly agreed to my using many of the firm's photographs reproduced here. This was a key factor in enabling the book to be produced at all. Don Sharp was a frequent source of information and inspiration, as he has been so often to so many others. Bari Logan and my wife Mary also provided much valuable assistance.

I am very grateful to them all for their help in creating this record of a famous and productive taxidermy business.

Contents

Source of pictures

Gerrards left little in the way of printed matter and there are few surviving employees. Inevitably the information base for this book has therefore been limited. However, there are substantial numbers of photographs available, making this more a picture book than a text book. Nevertheless, I hope it will serve as a record of a famous and productive firm of London taxidermists and natural history preparators.

Many of the photographs reproduced here were taken by the author, and I thank the museums and collectors who allowed me to do so. Gerrards also kept a set of photograph albums, featuring material prepared in the early 20th century. It is likely that the albums were shown to customers in order to suggest how their specimens might be set up and to indicate the extraordinary diversity of work that Gerrards could undertake. Some of these photographs were used in price lists, advertisements and other promotional material. Many of the images in those albums are now faded and too indistinct to be useful, but others have been reproduced here. Sadly none of the albums had captions or dates, so much interesting information has consequently been lost. Many of the photographs were taken in Gerrards own yard, with very little effort being made to screen out obtrusive elements of the background. This reduces their visual appeal, but adds considerably to their interest, as they show the context in which the taxidermists worked.

A third source of illustrations was a selection of Press photographs kept by the firm. Recent amalgamations of newspaper picture libraries have resulted in it being almost impossible to trace the copyright owner of these photographs unless they are held on file in one of the remaining libraries. Many of the prints have no attributions on them at all, nor any other clues as to when the picture might have been taken or by whom. Extensive efforts have been made to trace the ownership of these images, but often without success. I apologise if anyone feels that their rights have been infringed, and request that they contact the author. Two images were supplied by 'Mirrorpix' (Charles Gerrard with some tiger skin rugs in Ch 7 and also working on a trout, Ch 9). A taxidermist at work on a hippopotamus in Ch 3, and two that show employees preparing snake skeletons in Ch 10 are ©Hulton-Deutsch/CORBIS and James Stewart (Ch3) is ©John Springer Collection /CORBIS. Charles Gerrard and the model flea (Ch 10) is ©Getty images. Horace Owen (Ch 3) was photographed by Joan Gillet and the whale coccyx photograph (Ch 10) is reproduced by courtesy of Bari Logan.

Photographs taken by Gerrards were often only intended as 'record shots', with scant attention being paid to photographic niceties such as arranging a plain background or removing distracting objects from the field of view, such as the moving dog in this picture taken in Gerrard's yard. The background often adds interest to the photographs and also indicates the level of clutter that was associated with Gerrard's yard and sheds. The temptation to edit out the backgrounds has therefore been resisted in most cases.

The Gerrard Family

Chapter 1
The Gerrard Family

The Gerrard family tree is confusing and difficult to unravel. The confusion is excusable however, because for several generations the Gerrards followed a common practice of naming the first son after his father, thereby creating a succession of men all bearing the name 'Edward Gerrard'. A published account by Hillaby (1950), although seemingly detailed and accurate, is in fact misleading. Fortunately the family history has been unravelled by the two daughters of 'Mr Ted', Betty and Audrey. To remove ambiguity, they allocated numbers to the sequence of 'Edward Gerrards', and these are used here. The genealogy runs as below, focussing on those directly involved in the taxidermy business.

The Founder (Edward Gerrard 1st)

Edward Gerrard
1810 -1910

The original Edward Gerrard was born in Oxford in 1810 and moved to London with his parents. In 1836 he began work with the Zoological Society of London, as joint curator of the Society's museum. After five years he transferred to the British Museum, which he continued to serve for more than half a century. One of his first tasks was to assist in moving the collections from Montagu House to the new museum building in Bloomsbury. There he assisted Dr J E Gray, who particularly wished to build up representative collections of skeletons. These were stored in a cellar, where a fire was kept constantly burning to prevent them and their labels becoming mouldy as a result of the damp.

Working here, Edward Gerrard compiled a catalogue of specimens, using a tray on his knees as a table, there being so little space (Stearn, 1981). The catalogue of the collections was published and the specimens were later transferred to their own gallery at the new Natural History Museum in South Kensington. He was distressed when this display was dismantled. Apart from curating the osteology collections, Edward Gerrard had additional responsibilities for overseeing the accession of other vertebrate specimens. He was also keenly interested in general natural history and became an associate member of the Linnean Society of London. He was a friend of Charles Darwin too. Professionally he was widely known as a stalwart employee at the British Museum, and when he retired from there after 55 years, he received a special commendation from the Trustees.

Edward senior seems to have been a fit and healthy man who was rarely ill. Each day, regardless of the weather, he used to walk to work from Camden Town to Bloomsbury about 5km away, where the British Museum's natural history collections were held in those days.

By the time of the 1881 census he was a widower living with some younger relatives. He died on June 19th 1910, within a few weeks of his 101st birthday with his son, grandsons and his great-grandsons working for the business.

Edward Gerrard shortly before his 101st birthday.

Edward Gerrard 2nd

Edward Gerrard
1832 -1927

His son, Edward Gerrard 2nd, was born in about 1832 and joined his father in business, aged 18, when the family firm was set up in 1850. He was often referred to as Edward Gerrard Junior. According to an account by Hillaby (1950), Edward Gerrard Jr. left three sons Henry, Charles and Thomas Gerrard, and it was this Thomas that established the separate osteology and model making business, T. Gerrard & Co in the 1930s.

Edward Gerrard 3rd

The next Edward Gerrard was born in 1869 and married Minnie Emma Payne. She gave him eight children, several of whom later worked for the family business. The 1901 census shows Mr Edward Moore Gerrard, listed as a taxidermist, living with his wife Minnie and son of 11 months. The boy was Edward Francis Gerrard (Edward Gerrard 4th, 'Mr Ted'), who was born in 1900.

Edward Moore Gerrard
1869 -1906

Edward Gerrard 3rd died unexpectedly early, in 1906, aged only 37. Normally his eldest son (Edward 4th, 'Mr Ted') would have taken over, but he was only six years old at the time, so his uncle Harry (actually Henry Gerrard) ran the firm and was still in charge in 1938 according to a contemporary newspaper article. By the end of World War

Four generations of Gerrard taxidermists, with Edward Gerrard 1st seated at the front right, beside his great grandson, Edward 4th. Edward 3rd is at the left and Edward 2nd ('Edward Gerrard Jnr') is behind.

Two, he was still there, but by now rather deaf and nearly 80 years old. When he died, his heirs emigrated and sold the business to Edward 4th ('Mr Ted') and his brother Charles ('Mr Charles''). They had followed careers in the Navy, see below, and returned to civvy street to run the family firm jointly.

Charles Gerrard ('Mr Charles')

Charles Gerrard (1903-1971), photographed about 1970 by Bari Logan.

Charles Gerrard (also known as 'Charlie') was a cheery, friendly man, easy going and easy to get on with. He was always happy to comply with the needs of visiting press photographers, which is why so many of the contemporary pictures show him rather than anyone else.

Charles Gerrard in 1935 carrying an awkward bundle of goods through the yard. Charles was an easy going, cheerful sort of person who was evidently very willing to cooperate with visiting photographers, which is why he figures so frequently in contemporary newspapers and in the pages of this book.

In the post-war years, he was the firm's principal taxidermist. He was very versatile and apparently not dismayed by the variety and complexity of the many unfamiliar jobs that came his way. Although he served in the merchant navy he never went to either Africa or India, the source of so many hunting trophies, so his big game taxidermy had to be guided by photographs and visits to the London Zoo.

After the Second World War Charles worked in the family business at College Place, although he still lived in Rochester, while he waited for a posting at sea. This did not materialise, so he resigned from the Navy and joined the firm as a full time taxidermist, living for a while with his family in the damp basement at 61, College Pace. Charles was an accomplished artist, but it is not clear where he learned taxidermy. He was already

Charles Gerrard in the 1950s

familiar with the basics of what the family firm had done for so long, and he had worked there in the pre-war years. Presumably he learned on the job as he went along.

He also had a small collection of books. These included a set of Witherby's *Handbook of British Birds*, to which he often referred, a second hand copy of Oliver Davie's standard taxidermy manual (Davie, 1894) and *Our Country's Birds* by W.J. Gordon, which had a whole chapter giving useful measurements of birds. He also had a copy of the English edition of John Moyer's book *Practical Taxidermy* (Moyer, 1957), but evidently was already sufficiently experienced to feel moved to annotate the master's work in a critical fashion. In addition, the Gerrard library included an album of cigarette cards, showing colour illustrations of fish, and also the ninth edition of Rowland Ward's *Records of Big Game* (Dollman & Burlace, 1928), with its many helpful illustrations and measurements.

In the last two years of his life, Charles wrote a taxidermy book of his own. This began in 1970 as a plan to write what he called "a small pamphlet on taxidermy" motivated by a feeling that "most books I have read on the subject make the job far too complicated". He was aiming for teenage readers, presumably to provide advice for school leavers seeking a job in taxidermy. The book is written in a very direct style, almost like a tutorial session with the reader. It is a long series of practical tips and instructions, full of detailed observations based on personal experience (for example, the elegance of the eyelashes in a toucan and describing the difficulty of skinning the head of a shoveller by turning it inside out). The project expanded and became a 25,000 word manuscript, but writing it proved difficult for him, and he rewrote the first half three times, wrestling with an ancient and perverse typewriter, typing to the very edges of tiny sheets of paper (presumably in pursuit of economy). The text was submitted to David & Charles, but they declined to publish it, saying that it was *"too technical for beginners and too simple for experts"*.

The financial disaster (see Chapter 2) that resulted in closure of the firm, had left Charles penniless and without a home. He lost his house in North Finchley as it had been used to guarantee a bank loan to support the rug business. He retired to Sark in the Channel Islands, but later began to suffer from heart trouble and was hospitalised in 1971. Later that year he came to England, staying with his brother Ted in north London and doing odd jobs for Gerrard Hire Ltd. He planned to live on a houseboat, but had barely completed its purchase when he was taken ill again and died. Charles left two sons, Edward (Ted jnr, 1933 -) and Richard Henry (1939 -), who worked for a while as a young taxidermist in the family business.

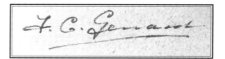

Edward Gerrard 4th ('Mr Ted')

Edward Francis Gerrard married and had two daughters, Elisabeth and Audrey. He and his brother Charles had attended Dartmouth naval college after the First World War, and he remained a Navy engineer, while Charles worked in the aircraft industry for a time and later served in the Navy. Ted was somewhat more reserved and formal than his brother, and more conscious of being 'The Boss' of the family firm. In fact he did not take on the business until late in life as his uncle Harry was already running it. After the end of the Second World War, Ted and Charles bought the business from

Edward Gerrard 4th
1900 -1976, in about 1920

Harry, who then emigrated with his children to Rhodesia. Ted travelled in each day from Rochester, then bought a house in Woodside Park (North London) in the 1950s. He was a very practical man and set about repairing the dilapidated workshop premises in Camden Town, by now suffering from years of neglect and wartime shortage of materials.

Although Ted was not especially interested in taxidermy, he became a very skilled and ingenious model maker and made a long series of tailors manikins for use in displaying ladies clothing in shop windows. Animal models, plaster casts, special exhibition models, all sorts of items were produced, continuing the impressive versatility of the Gerrard family firm and helping to diversify its output and thereby reduce its dependence on taxidermy. The firm also made many of the mechanical dummy 'hares' used at local greyhound races, comprising a rubber body covered with real fur.

The two brothers ran the operation until its closure in 1967. After the collapse of the main company, Ted worked part time for Gerrard Hire Ltd, assisting with putting up shelves and doing other odd jobs. He died in 1976.

'Mr Ted' in the Gerrard showroom in 1950

The Taxidermy Company

Chapter 2
The Taxidermy Company

Edward Gerrard 1st (1810-1910) set up the family taxidermy business 'Edward Gerrard and Sons' in 1850, whilst still employed by the British Museum, and took on his eldest son to run it. This is the date stated for the foundation of the firm on most of its literature (although a later date was sometimes given). Early on, the business was based at the family home, 54 Queen's St, Camden Town (1870-79) in north London, but later moved to the yard behind 61 College Place, also in Camden Town.

Camden Town was close to the London Zoo, with all its interesting animals, and itself a focus for so many of the zoological luminaries of the day. Very early on, well before the end of the nineteenth century, the nearby Gerrard workshops had become famous as a place where hunters, travellers and naturalists could meet and exchange or sell specimens. Thus, the juxtaposition of zoo and taxidermist must have proved very advantageous all round, and certainly ensured that a supply of interesting dead animals was readily available not far away. Many

Gerrards also had premises round the corner in Royal College Street, where these children posed for some newspaper photographs.

From the early days, Gerrards purchased specimens, like this gorilla skin and skull, from zoos, professional collectors and hunters. They also bought zoological curios at auction (like the giant Aepyornis egg in the background).

valuable specimens came from there, and some of the individual animals were famous in their own right.

During the heyday of British taxidermy, from about 1880 until the First World War, Gerrards was a thriving

In time, Gerrards became sufficiently well known that even mail to "the man who stuffs animals, London" was still delivered to the right place. The Post Office was easily able to guess where it was meant to go and could add the correct address.

EDWARD GERRARD & SONS ———— ESTD. 1850

Telephone
Telegrams } EUSton 2765

1.— STUDIOS - 61, College Place, N.W.1.
2.— MORNINGTON CRESCENT nearest Tube Station.
3.— Camden Town Tube Station.
   Buses 27, 127, 29, 39, 24, 63.

SHOWROOM ————
and STUDIOS ————

**61, COLLEGE PLACE
CAMDEN TOWN
LONDON, N.W.1**

A brochure, issued in 1938, showed where to find Gerrards

business, although they were in competition with dozens of other taxidermists, large and small. In the 1930s there were five or six employees whose wives often helped out by doing the office work. The business remained operational on a small scale during the Second World War providing employment for a few elderly staff. There was little demand for taxidermy, but some specimens were hired out for use in wartime propaganda and instructional films. Gerrards even issued a brief price list in 1942, offering a mounted blackbird or a waxwing for 15/6d or a bittern for £3. Soon after the War, prices increased and a waxwing (perhaps the same one) was now 18/6d and a blackbird was £1/2/6d. By 1947 a mounted blackbird cost £2/2/6d, a waxwing (perhaps still the same one!) was £2/17/6d and a badger was priced at £8/15/-. (an explanation of prices is given in Chapter 4).

Throughout its time in business, the company offered a wide range of services, not just taxidermy. In particular, they specialised in supplying articulated skeletons. The Founder himself had been a skilled osteological preparator and headed notepaper dated 1906 shows that Edward Gerrard "Taxidermists and articulators" was supplying skeletal specimens to the Dublin Museum.

Making (and selling) natural history models was also established early on, and by the 1930s a wide range of such products was available for purchase by schools and museums.

Contemporary price lists and advertisements feature comparative models of brains, and the embryonic development of the chick. These, and models showing development and life cycle of the frog, proved popular teaching aids. They were easy to see, being several times life size, and also readily available from a classroom cupboard at all times of the year, unlike the real thing. Other models featured insect life cycles and species that were of economic importance. The market for these models was substantial because comparative anatomy and embryology of specified species remained the foundation stones of biological studies in both schools and also at universities. Many hundreds of sets were probably produced, although once purchased, they tended to be durable and could be used for decades without needing to be replaced.

Examples of headed notepaper, showing the various services available.

61, College Place, Camden Town, N.W.

P. H. P. Powell Cotton, Esq.   London, Oct. 15th 1899

To Edward Gerrard & Sons,

Taxidermists and Articulators.

WORK FOR MUSEUMS AND INSTITUTIONS A SPECIALITY.   SPECIMENS SUPPLIED.

Skins, Heads, Rugs, and Natural History Specimens Mounted in the best style.

Medals Awarded at the Dublin, Moscow, Calcutta, Fishery, Indian and Colonial, and Adelaide Exhibitions.

		£	s	d
1898	To dressing Rabbits & making rug		15	
Nov.	To mounting an Elephants head & modelling tusks	10		
"	Packing	10		
"	mounting 3 Arnee Buffalo heads	15		
"	2 Gour	9		
"	Packing		15	
"	dressing 2 Gour skins lining & trimming	5		
		£41	—	—
By Balance of former a/c	£42.5.6			
" Skins as agreed (15.4.99)	118 – 0 – 0			
	£160 5 6			
Balance due Oct 18.99	£119 5 6			
for P. H. P. Powell Cotton Esq.				

EDWARD GERRARD & SONS,
Naturalists,
TAXIDERMISTS & ARTICULATORS.

Skins, Heads, Rugs, & Natural History Specimens Mounted.

Medals awarded at the Dublin, Moscow, Calcutta, Fishery, Indian and Colonial, and Adelaide Exhibitions.

61, College Place,
Camden Town,
London, Augt. 24th 1898

Headed notepaper from the mid 1920s (above) and pre- First World War (below)

For
MUSEUMS
——
Taxidermy
Osteology
Zoology
Botany
Dissections
Injections
Microscope
Slides
Instruments
Apparatus
Glass Jars
Tanks
Preservatives
Stains
Specimens
Models
Charts
School Loan
Collection
Nature
Study

E. GERRARD & SONS
61 COLLEGE PLACE, CAMDEN TOWN, LONDON

For
SCHOOLS
——
**Evolution
series of
Brains**
◄(as illustration)
Worm
Crayfish
Cockroach
Snail
Amphioxus
Codfish
Dogfish
Frog
Lizard
Pigeon
Rabbit
Kangaroo
Sheep
Cat
Dog
Mole or Bat
Lemur
Monkey

PRINTED IN GREAT BRITAIN BY JARROLD & SONS, LIMITED
LONDON AND NORWICH

An advertisement for model brains. Initially the various types of models were made from plaster of Paris, but later on other materials were pressed into use.

Complementing these teaching sets were some models of animals that do not lend themselves to successful taxidermy, notably reptiles and amphibians. These were popular with schools, but were also frequently purchased by museums wanting to display local British wildlife. In 1951, a coloured plaster cast of an adder, life-sized, would have cost £3.

By the early 1930s, Thomas Gerrard was running an almost autonomous division, concentrating on skeletal preparations and model making, using some additional sheds (later demolished) adjacent to the Gerrard main yard. In fact the osteology and educational models were sufficiently popular that it was possible for Thomas Gerrard to break away and set up his own business in 1938, specialising in just this type of work. Later he added various other teaching materials and T. Gerrard & Co became the market leader for such biological supplies.

The relationship between the two businesses is unclear. The establishment of a competing operation, albeit within the family, cannot have been warmly welcomed back in Camden Town. However, the yard at College Place was too small to expand this line of work, so business opportunities could be better exploited by moving the modelling and supply of teaching materials

to another site. Nevertheless, models continued to be made in College Place, as well as by T. Gerrard & Co. Moreover, the latter also supplied taxidermy on a small scale, so there was overlap in their products and probably a degree of competition developed between the two firms.

Whilst Gerrards did have some specialists, jobs were often given to whoever was available. Some of the taxidermists had to work on fish and birds as well as mammals. In fact Gerrard's relied a lot on the diverse skills of their employees. Improvisation seems to have been foremost among their talents. Gerrard's were always distinctive in offering a very wide range of products, far more diverse than any other British taxidermists. Their output included not just birds, mammals, fish and reptiles, but also models, skulls and skeletons, rugs, animal furniture and ornaments and even shoes and fancy leather bags. Latterly, there was also a Hire Division. It was this unique breadth of output that made Gerrards so interesting and so different from other contemporary taxidermists. Diversity was also probably a commercial necessity given the dominant market position of Rowland Ward Ltd since the late 19th century, with their large factory in Kentish Town and prominent shop in fashionable Piccadilly. Ward's were a very powerful competitor in the limited market for large scale taxidermy. Yet, at the same time, there were scores of minor taxidermy businesses that competed effectively

Plaster cast of an adder, painted to create natural colours and patterns

for commissions to mount birds, fox masks and perform other small-scale taxidermy work. In the late nineteenth century, London alone had more than a dozen flourishing taxidermy businesses operating simultaneously, plus many others too small to be listed in trade directories. Gerrard's were squeezed between the two fields of taxidermy work, large and small.

Nevertheless, they occupied a successful commercial niche, and even did taxidermy for other firms. The Army and Navy stores passed on some work and Gerrards also did jobs for Rowland Ward Ltd, especially rugs because Gerrard's had a pinking machine, to produce the wrinkled felt edging used to trim animal skin rugs, whereas Wards had not acquired such a device.

Space was a limiting factor, so the firm could never have had more than about a dozen or so employees in total.In the mid 1960s There were seven taxidermists, including Charles Gerrard, his son Dick and Don Sharp (who was a couple of years younger). Another of the taxidermists was Bill Dwyer, who always wore a hat and was very secretive, covering his work so that no one could see what he was doing. He had left the firm to fight in the Boer War, but returned and was still working for Gerrards in the 1950s mounting trophies, although by now he was about 80 years old. There was also Horace Owen, another taxidermist and long-time employee, who

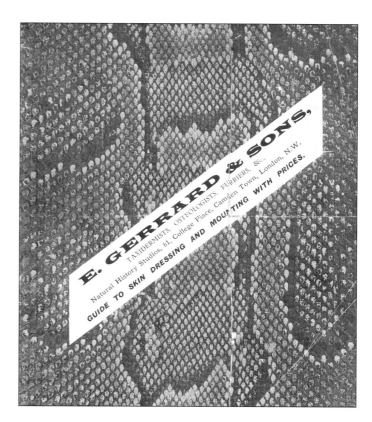

A brochure marked 1932. Its 11 pages (26 x 20 cm) cover mostly skins, rugs and furniture. A small section offers things made from rhino hide (including tables and bowls). The last page gives directions for sending specimens, with some incongruous remarks and photographs to fill the remaining space.

Below: (with a sample page) is a small (19 x 15cm) brochure of 20 pages dated 1951. Another copy from Gerrard's office was dated 1947 by hand.

Edw. Gerrard & Sons

TAXIDERMISTS

FURRIERS

MODELLERS

NATURALISTS

ESTABLISHED A CENTURY

NATURAL HISTORY STUDIOS

61 COLLEGE PLACE

CAMDEN TOWN, N.W.I

Telephone Number: EUSTON 2765

Mounting of Birds supplied by Customer

On imitation earth base, or base and perch.

These prices only apply to freshly dead birds, or skins. The nostrils and mouths should be plugged with cotton wool and care should be taken not to damage the plumage when packing. We cannot give a price for every bird, but as our charges are governed mainly by the size of the specimen the following will act as a guide.

	£	s.	d.
Wren, Humming Bird		12	6
Sparrow...		15	0
Canary, Budgerigar ...		18	6
Starling, Thrush ...	1	2	6
Jay, Little Owl ...	1	7	6
Grouse	1	15	0
Herring Gull, Pheasant	1	18	6
Domestic Fowl	2	17	6
Penguin	3	5	0
King Penguin	4	0	0

There is a small extra charge for mounting the bird with outstretched wings. We also make "Cabinet Skins" from customers' specimens, for study purposes, at a charge of from 5/- for small birds to £1 for large birds.

A selection of advertisements

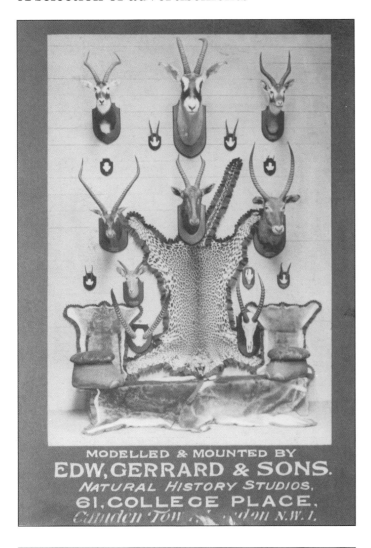

Top left: advertising panel, undated, perhaps never used.
Above: an advertisement in the Kenya & Uganda Guide, 1939;
Below: advertisements in the London Zoo guide for 1907 (far left)
and 1930 (centre).

Few of Gerrard's price lists were illustrated and none
were dated. Three of the most comprehensive are shown
on pp 13 & 15. They were originally kept by the
manager of Rowland Ward Ltd, and they were dated by
him in pencil.

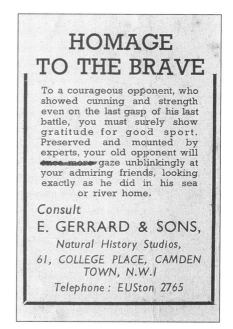

Above, with a sample page below, is a brochure from 1921. It consists of 14 illustrated pages 20 x 28cm. It includes 2 pages covering heads, skulls and horns, 4 pages on feet and hooves, 3 pages on tusks and claws, 1 page on fish and birds and 1 page each on rhino hide tables and skin dressing. The number of pages devoted to each area of activity is probably a fair reflection of the relative diversity within each of these categories of Gerrard's products.

Above: spoof April 1st advertisement placed in The Field.

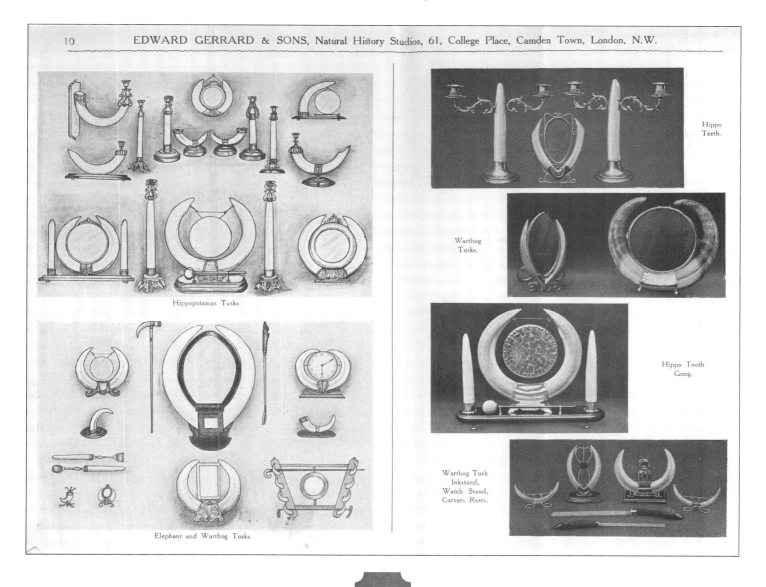

did dogs and game heads. Ted Paul worked in the bird section, once completing 36 mallard cabinet skins for Harrod's in a single day. He was very short, but somehow used to race penny farthing bikes. In addition there was an office secretary and 'Mr. Ted' (Edward Gerrard 4th). He was a skilled model maker and also ran the commercial aspects of the business. It seems that full use was thus made of the various talents within the family operation, and the staff were also encouraged to rise to the many challenges offered. It was a happy and creative working environment.

No women actually worked as taxidermists, but several were employed as furriers at various times and also as office assistants. They included Audrey Gerrard who worked there for 8 years (1955-1963) among the other staff, dealing with the letters and invoices and a multiplicity of general jobs. She and another woman seem to have fitted fairly comfortably into what might otherwise have been a very male-oriented workplace, but she was the boss's daughter and the other woman (Mary) 'could hold her own with anyone'.

In the post-war years, Gerrard's output was far more varied than if Charles and Ted had both worked only as taxidermists. However, pursuing a 'Jack of all trades' business strategy does have its dangers, notably of being 'master of none' and gaining a reputation for sub-standard work. But, after the War, there was relatively little competition, so this mattered less than previously. In any case, some of Gerrard's work was of very high quality indeed, but the demand for it was waning.

By the 1960s, taxidermy had ceased to be the firm's main activity, with model making being more important to the business. Even the manufacture of shop window manikins became a significant source of income. As the demand for taxidermy dwindled, diversity represented a commercial strength for Gerrards and probably helped the company to survive longer than it might otherwise have done. By the time Gerrards finally closed down, in 1967, the London Post Office directories showed only one other taxidermy business (Rowland Ward Ltd) still operating in the capital.

The end of Gerrards

By the early 1960s, there was an increasing awareness among the public, especially those interested in wildlife, of the need to conserve the living rather than preserve the dead. Big game hunting, a major prop of the taxidermy business, was becoming expensive and increasingly restricted by conservation legislation. It was also becoming practically more difficult, with the loss of easy access to the Empire as many former hunting

grounds became independent countries and no longer employed British personnel whose spare time would be spent hunting. Hunting was also giving way to filming and photography as a newly fashionable challenge that was focussed on wildlife. Slowly taxidermy and its products fell from favour in the domestic market. Most museums already had all the specimens they wanted and with depleted purchase grants could not afford more anyway. Moreover, changing public tastes encouraged them towards new exhibits featuring interactive displays, artistic interpretive material and models rather than taxidermy. For all these reasons, taxidermists found it increasingly difficult to survive commercially, even the largest and best of them. Gerrards survived longer than most.

Addresses taken from London Trade Directories

1870-1879:
Edward Gerrard, 54, Queen's St, Camden Town

1902-1905:
Edward Gerrard & Sons, College Place, Camden Town

1906-1960:
Edward Gerrard & Sons, 61 College Place

1930-1938:
Edward Gerrard & Sons, 2 Camden Studios

1930-1939:
Edward Gerrard & Sons, 4 Camden Studios

1935-1938:
Edward Gerrard & Sons, 1 Camden Studios

1935-1938:
Edward Gerrard & Sons, 3 Camden Studios

NB- 'Camden Studios' was also 61 College Place.
Telephone numbers at College Place were
EUSton 2765 from at least 1938 until the 1960s.
NORth 2358- in 1920 & 1932
This can sometimes help in dating labelled specimens.

Edward Gerrard & Sons did not own the yard in which their workshops were sited. Instead, they had a ninety nine year lease from the Church Commissioners. When the whole area was scheduled for redevelopment as part of a new housing scheme, the firm accepted Camden Council's offer of relocation and vacated both the yard and 61 College Place to allow for demolition. They moved briefly to 1 Ferdinand Place in Chalk Farm, NW1, before finally closing down. The west side of

College Place became part of a block of flats and the old yard and workshop site is now a series of lock-up garages and a parking area.

According to Herriott (1968) the end came in 1965, but this probably represents the cessation of taxidermy work. The formal winding up of Edward Gerrard & Sons did not happen until 1967.

The rug division survived briefly but suffered a final blow in a complex deal involving a large batch of goat skins. It is difficult now to establish exactly what happened, but some kind of deal was set up that went badly wrong. The skins were paid for, but were then stuck on a boat in the Suez Canal when that was closed due to the Arab-Israeli war in 1967, and they never reached London. The company's finances were too fragile to sustain such a blow and the business was put in the hands of the receivers, Corke Gully. The collapse was very sudden and a bitter disappointment to the employees. Worse, Charles lost his house, which he had used as surety to underwrite the purchase of the skins. Ted's home was only saved because it was owned by his wife. The Hire Service was hived off as a separate company (Gerrard Hire Ltd), trading from the old store at 85 Royal College Street, just around the corner from College Place.

A Gerrard pony. The boy is real, the son of Ann Bradshaw, secretary to the business, 1952-55

College Place and Gerrard's yard as they are now.

Above: Looking south into College Place as it is today. No. 61 and the entrance to Gerrard's yard were on the right hand corner by the lamp post. All that (west) side of the street is now occupied by a block of flats.
Below: Looking north-east from within what was Gerrard's yard.

The flats now occupy the position of no. 61, but the fig tree that flourished in the garden is still there. The new brick wall was built with a curve to accommodate it. The tree is visible in a picture of an elephant in the yard (see Chapter 3). The yard itself is now a car park and lock up garages.

Gerrard's Workshops

Chapter 3
Gerrard's Workshops

Turning into College Place from the north, on the right hand side was the Gerrard family home at number 61. This was a three storey house, typical of many in North London. Several of the rooms were used for the business and it had a basement too. Although this had been the family home in the pre-war years, after the war both the proprietors, Charles and Ted Gerrard, lived elsewhere.

Two brick pillars, painted white, stood either side of a narrow alleyway adjacent to the house. They supported double wooden doors, painted dark green. The pillars were at one time surmounted by a pair of rubber penguins. During the 1950s, and probably for long before that, a wooden signboard spanned the alley. This formed a 'V' shape with two faces, each announcing "E. Gerrard & Sons, Natural History Studios". This was the entrance to the alley that led to the workshops behind.

This alley and the atmospheric workshops formed the backdrop to part of the 1956 film *The Man Who Knew Too Much*. This was a remake by Alfred Hitchcock of his own 1934 film of the same name. It starred James Stewart and Doris Day. The film's hero, Dr Ben Mc-Kenna, is seen visiting a London taxidermist called Ambrose Chappell. The film shows general clutter, with a lion's foreparts in the middle of the floor and various heads (including a rhino and many fox masks), hanging on the wall. Old bottles, a shovel and coils of wire are also evident. This is as it would have been at Gerrards, there was no need to recreate the scene in a studio.

In the film, 'Dr McKenna' is seen visiting Gerrards yard, relabelled 'Ambrose Chappell'. He has an aggressive interview with the boss, surrounded by bits of half finished work hanging on the walls and a taxidermist stuffing wood wool into a leopard skin. A fight develops and the taxidermist tries to keep his leopard out of the way, while another attempts to rescue a stuffed sawfish. Various other staff wrestle with James Stewart, presumably paid up members of the Actors' union rather than real taxidermists. In the melee, the hero gets his hand caught briefly in the open mouth of a mounted tiger. It's all very dramatic and weird, no doubt why Hitchcock selected this location to film, but completely irrelevant to the story. 'Dr McKenna' had in fact misunderstood something he heard from a dying man and went looking for a fellow called Ambrose Chappell, when he should have been looking for a chapel of a different kind!

The alleyway ran alongside the house for about 20 metres, then turned left and led into a long yard that lay behind the gardens of College Place. A high brick wall surrounded the yard, within which a series of six large, single-storey wood and brick sheds housed the Gerrard workshops for decades. These might once have been stables or light industry workshops. They each had a high slate roof over dirty yellow brick walls, typical of north London. The first shed had large doors, painted dark green.

© *John Springer Collection/ CORBIS*
James Stewart, seen visiting 'Ambrose Chappell', whose sign is simply a printed sheet pasted over the Gerrard name on their own signboard. The number 61 (College Place) was unchanged on the brick pillars at the entrance to the alley. (A Press photo of James Stewart signing autographs outside the Gerrard alley, with their own signboard visible, can be seen on the MPTV website, http://www.netropolisusa.biz/scripts, image archives no. 5372-0027)

Various other lean-to sheds made of wood and corrugated iron added to the storage space available, and a hand cart stood ready to collect and deliver specimens. In the narrow space between the outer wall and the sheds there were maceration tanks in which skulls and bones could be rotted free of flesh before cleaning. Odd piles of skulls, antlers and horns were to be seen here and there, and large stacks of them were heaped up in the space between the workshops and the yard's outer wall.

It was in the big sheds (or 'shops' as they were sometimes known) that different aspects of the business were pursued. The sheds were actually quite large, but always very cluttered. They had large windows, glazed with small panes set in iron frames. The glass was usually dirty, giving a low- level of diffuse light, which reflected off the walls that had once been white. A few electric light bulbs hanging from the roof, some screened by enamelled iron lampshades, provided additional illumination. Sometimes a wireless would be audible, tuned to the BBC's Home Service.

The high walls surrounding the yard shielded the buildings from the sun so they tended to be cool inside, even during the summer. In winter the workshops were cold and dingy, although large iron 'tortoise' stoves served to generate a little warmth. A Persian cat sat on a shelf above one of the stoves and frequently got singed. Visitors to the premises always found it disturbing to see some cats scuttling about the yard, whilst others sat motionless on shelves and work benches, staring blankly with their glassy eyes.

A corner of the showroom.

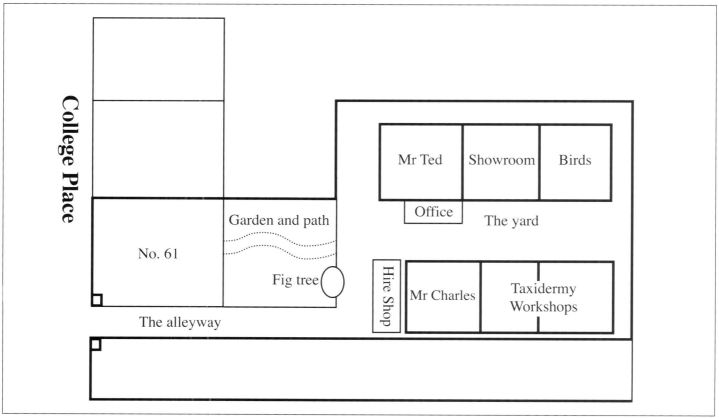

Sketch map of Gerrard's yard as it was during the early 1960s.

The Showroom

One of these buildings, 'the showroom', was intended to impress customers and visitors. It contained an arresting and jumbled display of taxidermy and general curios including a giant reconstructed egg of the extinct elephant bird (*Aepyornis*) , various bits of animal furniture (notably a circular mirror suspended between hippo tusks), the head of a rogue elephant, a baby camel and a selection of peacock feathers, all of which are visible in various contemporary newspaper photographs. Unlike at Rowland Ward's taxidermy workshop, there was a positive attitude towards publicity. Photographers were frequent and welcome visitors, so the showroom and its contents were well documented in the popular Press of the day. This building was the nearest that Gerrards had to a front office. Visitors would often arrive at the yard and wander about until someone appeared from out of one of the workshops and offered to help. There was no proper reception area or shop counter. Gerrard's yard was more like a factory than a shop.

There were some big maceration bins just outside the showroom building in which the flesh on skulls and bones was allowed decompose until they could be cleaned up fully and bleached. This must have created significant odours, especially during warm weather. However, a crusty scum soon develops on such tanks, sealing in the smell until such times as the tank is

The buildings were poorly lit and full of extraordinary creatures. The bars on the windows were meant to deter thieves, but any casual burglar breaking in here at night would have had an unforgettable surprise!

disturbed by someone adding material or attempting to remove whatever lies submerged within its nauseous depths. The smell could then easily escape and must sometimes have been quite pungent. Indeed the smell was said to be one of the more memorable aspects of a visit to Gerrard's yard. Small wonder that there were complaints from the police quarters beyond the boundary wall, concerning the sights and smells of neighbourhood taxidermy.

The other buildings were allocated to various workshop functions, with three being used for taxidermy in later years under the eye of 'Mr Charles'. One was devoted to work on birds. The remaining buildings housed other jobs, including model making, and there was also a large store of glass domes. The showroom and office were under the supervision of 'Mr Ted'. At one time rugs were made here too, but this work was later transferred to the house.

Between the yard and the house was a small garden, entered via a tall gate. Here cricket was played during summer lunch breaks, and various bodies were also buried there from time to time (see below). From the garden, clerical and senior staff were allowed into the house, whose dank basement was occupied by Frank the caretaker, and where some of the Gerrard family had

Typical Gerrard products in the showroom.

Above: The showroom in 1950, with a vast selection of typical Gerrard products.

lived for a while. The ground floor was used as the firm's office and the first floor formed the rug making shop. The upper (second) floor was used as a storeroom. There was also a store round the corner at 85, Royal College Street, where customer's specimens were hung on the walls and stacked on the floor to await collection.

Disposal of decaying remains must have been a problem, particularly where larger specimens had been skinned in the yard rather than sent in as skins prepared and dried elsewhere. A letter from Gerrards to Bowdler Sharpe at the British Museum explained that a substantial bill for preserving a foal, included £1/1/- for carriage and 10/- expenses "for getting rid of the body". At least once a week, dustmen would remove large amounts of rubbish, including flesh and other unwanted organic material, perhaps encouraged by a generous tip at Christmas, something they would never do today. Other material, including bones that needed to be retrieved after decomposition of flesh, was buried at the back of the garden. Here grew a particularly luxuriant fig tree, no doubt benefitting from the additional nutrients that were periodically interred

among its roots. When the workshops were demolished and replaced by a housing development, the back garden wall was rebuilt with a sweeping curve in it to encompass the tree rather than remove it. Although the tree was subsequently cut back fairly drastically, it was still flourishing in 2003, more than 35 years after its last 'meal' of taxidermy refuse.

'Mr Ted' in the showroom, with the rogue elephant head very prominently displayed.

The yard itself was usually pretty cluttered. This photograph of a dead porpoise shows a stack of hippo and antelope skulls against the wall behind. The Dall sheep and the elephant tusks were photographed among packing cases and a porter's trolley, although some tidying up was done before photographing the elephant in the yard. The garden fig tree (see previous page) is above its head

The workshops were always a bit dank and musty due to the general dampness and lack of adequate heating and ventilation. Superimposed on this general aura were the smells of methylated spirits, varnish, benzene and other solvents. There were also biological odours, such as the acrid smell of foxes that had been chased by the hunts and deposited days later with the taxidermists. Occasionally the smell of putrid flesh would hang in the air and some of the fox head trophies arriving in the warm days of autumn were said to be "almost capable of walking in by themselves". The worst case of putrefaction was probably an Aldabran giant tortoise to be set up for display at Downe House, Darwin's old home. Tortoises have an unpleasant smell anyway, even when fresh. This one arrived from a zoo, via the Royal College of Surgeons, frozen solid. It then had to be thawed out, a process that always hastens decay. It took several odorous days to remove all the flesh from inside the carapace, by which time the job had become decidedly unsavoury.

Working conditions in Gerrard's yard were not ideal. Illumination was through dirty windows, supplemented by bare light bulbs. Tools and bits of partially completed work were everywhere. The benches sometimes got so cluttered that staff ended up using an orange box at the end of the bench to provide a clear flat surface. Well into the 1950s, Gerrards continued to use arsenic paste (made up by Charles) as a skin preservative and insecticide, especially on stored skins. Various other chemicals now seen as hazardous were also used in large quantity. For example, benzene (a carcinogen) was used a lot for cleaning skins after they had been washed in water. After soaking in the benzene, skins were shaken up with granular magnesium carbonate to dry them and fluff out the fur. The powder and the benzene were blown out in the yard. Despite the many potential hazards, from which modern safety legislation protects today's employees, there seem to have been few accidents at Gerrards and none form part of the family's collective memory. Moreover, despite the use of arsenic and a generally informal approach to hygiene, several of the employees worked there well beyond normal retiring age and enjoyed an above-average lifespan. At least two taxidermists still worked for the firm when they were over 80 years old. Its founder lived to be 100.

Several photographs of Bill Smith and Charles Gerrard show them working in white shirts with collar and tie. Woolly pullovers were the norm in winter, seemingly a rather unsuitable garb for a taxidermist. Bill often dressed in a tweed jacket too, and hats were sometimes worn indoors as well. Although Charles and some of the others usually wore a storekeeper's overall, most of the staff would have worn the same clothes to go home in on the bus, more or less regardless of what they had been working on during the day. Nevertheless, dress was still

This Borzoi was tied to a door handle, not to prevent it from running away, but because it was badly mounted and would never stand up on its own.

Not all of Gerrard's work was done at College Place. Here, the Pinfolds (father and son) tackle a habitat group of beavers being installed in a museum, the taxidermy having been done back at the workshop. G.W. Pinfold worked for Gerrards 1920-1930, then transferred to the Powell Cotton Museum where he worked until his death in 1940.

Every available bit of space indoors was filled with specimens awaiting collection (above) and in the actual workshops there was scarcely room to move.

The taxidermists work benches were always full of jobs and materials, leaving little room to eat lunch.

somewhat more formal than we might expect in a modern workplace and Ted was dismayed when Joan Gillett turned up to work for the Hire Division wearing trousers instead of a skirt (although this was a practical necessity given the draughty state of the hire division's premises!).

The staff

The staff arrived early in the morning and got on with their work. They drank tea and ate lunch at their workbench, clearing space among the jobs in hand. There was little time or reason to think or talk about anything other than what they were doing. In summer, they occasionally played ball games in the garden of 61 College Place during the lunch break. Smoking could have been a hazard, with inflammable material lying about and Charles Gerrard did smoke occasionally, although not indoors. Few of the other staff smoked at all. The hours were long and the work was sometimes challenging and disagreeable, but the general atmosphere was quiet and congenial.

Basically, Gerrards was a family firm, and treated its staff in a friendly manner without undue formality. Don Sharp warmly recalled that 'Mr. Charles' treated him like a son and later regarded him almost as an equal out of respect for his work. "He was a real gentleman".

Customers did sometimes come to the workshops, perhaps to offer thanks for jobs well done or to discuss new orders, but the workers were little involved, being preoccupied with their own work.

Nobody actually taught newcomers. They were just expected to pick up the multifarious skills that were needed as they went along. The taxidermists did not make much use of books or photographs for reference, but they did sometimes go to the zoo nearby. Charles kept an eye on things, but otherwise the workers were left to themselves to get on with their jobs with the minimum of fuss and interference. This relaxed atmosphere is probably one reason why the output from Gerrards varied so much in quality. Some of their taxidermy products were excellent, even by modern standards, and probably reflect happy creativity at work. However, some of the output was pretty dreadful, again perhaps reflecting the lack of pressure put on staff to maintain high standards.

The nature of the work varied a lot, and this must have been both a constant stimulation and frequent challenge. The taxidermists were expected to cope with all sorts of tasks. One week it might be rhino feet, hacking out the bones and gristle and filling the skin with silver sand. The skin was warmed by immersion in hot water and a rounded wooden block would then be pressed into the feet by hand (not by hydraulic machinery). Weights were piled on and left for weeks for the feet to dry. This was hard physical work.

At other times a taxidermist had less demanding tasks, but would be expected to produce two mounted birds or two fox heads per day as the norm. These would be hung up to dry then finished later in batches. Sometimes there would be piles of skins to deal with, other times skulls

Bottom left: Alan wears a storekeeper's overall, as does Bill Smith (top left), although in the picture above, the man is simply wearing his everyday clothes, a tweed jacket, pullover and tie.

Above: packing a batch of big cat skin rugs or (below) modelling a hippo's gums was all in a day's work for staff like young Davies, photographed here in 1958. (©Hulton - Deutsch/CORBIS)

Ernie Shrosbree has his trilby hat on whilst brushing out the fur of a giant panda skin. Several of Gerrard's taxidermists wore hats, perhaps to keep out the cold.

or fish needed treatment. Certain staff specialised in these tasks, but the demand for inventiveness and originality must also have fostered the development of wide-ranging talents.

Periodically there would be large batches of work to complete, for example as a customer's trophies all arrived from the docks, following a hunting expedition to Africa. From the autumn onwards there would also be scores of fox heads to set up as hunting trophies. At certain times of the year large numbers of these would be standing around drying. One job not done on site was the tanning of skins. Large pelts were sent to Fisher's to be tanned, smaller ones required for mounting animals such as foxes and cats were not tanned at all.

There were often many antelope heads hanging on the walls, waiting for the rest of a large consignment to be ready for shipment to the customer. Gerrard's rarely bought in ready-made manikins for mounting trophy heads, but made them in house from papier maché and wire, another specialised job that men needed to learn.

Horace Owen- Gerrard's last taxidermist

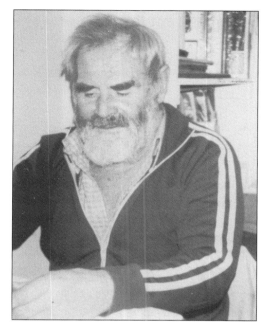

Horace Owen, about 1980.

Harold Frederick ('Horace') Owen was one of the key employees, serving Gerrards for a total of more than half a century. He was born in 1916. He lived all his life in the Tottenham area of north London and joined Gerrards as a school leaver, aged about 15, after seeing the work of his uncle Paul, a specialist in bird taxidermy who also worked for the firm. Horace was a taciturn and introspective man, who kept himself to himself. He was rather shy and withdrawn, especially with strangers, and although self-taught in wildlife matters, he was very knowledgeable. He was happiest with his tent, camped out alone somewhere where he could go swimming and watch wildlife, skinning the odd carcass he found dead by the road. He was also an intrepid cyclist and could sometimes be persuaded to tell stories of collecting specimens from the London Zoo and wheeling them back to the workshops on his handlebars. As with many of the old time taxidermists he was often reluctant to give away the secrets of his trade. He served as a general taxidermist until the outbreak of hostilities in 1939, then worked on building sites during the war, demolishing buildings damaged during the blitz. He rejoined Gerrards after the war and then worked continuously until taxidermy ceased. He was offered a job with the Hire company, but for six years he insisted on working only as a freelance. After that he agreed to join the payroll, perhaps having been suspicious of the new arrangements and new (female) boss.

He continued to mount specimens long after retirement age, adding to the stock held by the hire company. He did not specialise in a particular field of taxidermy, but was able to mount any specimen that was to hand, large or small, mammal or bird. He prepared many thousands of specimens during his working life. Fox masks were a frequent item and he could sometimes be seen with up to fifteen of them hanging up around his bench in various states of completion. Horace was one of the few taxidermists who would happily undertake work on pets and he produced some excellent mounted dogs and cats. His mounted dogs were particularly life-like. Domestic dogs are difficult to prepare as many often have excessive amounts of fat on their body by the time they die. Sometimes customers expressed themselves disappointed, but Horace thought that was because they were unsure they wanted the job done in the first place. Sometimes the animals would not be collected and would then be added to the Hire stock. In time the collection included more than 30 dogs, which proved to be very popular with photographers and film makers owing to their uncanny natural appearance.

Horace mounted many of the larger mammal specimens from dried skins that had been kept in store and he helped to build up the large and comprehensive stock for hire. He also did some taxidermy for customers of the Hire company, including badgers, foxes, pheasants and owls, to the delight of many members of the public who experienced considerable difficulty finding a practising taxidermist in the late 1960s and early 1970s. However, as he got older he found it harder to continue with his taxidermy. In 1989 he brought in the last of his work prior to taking his long summer holiday. He was not seen again.

A koala Horace mounted from an old skin.

Don Sharp

Don Sharp talking to the Author whilst setting up a badger.

Don Sharp skinned his first bird when he was about ten years old, inspired by a visit to the Rothschild Museum at Tring. It was a blackbird, killed by a passing car, but too good to be allowed to just rot away. Over the next three years he received considerable encouragement from his mother and also his schoolteacher, who arranged an interview for him at Gerrards. He took to London two suitcases containing some of his own specimens (including a fox, hedgehog and some small birds) and showed them to Charles Gerrard, displaying them on a table made of rhino hide. He was asked to begin work immediately, but Don explained that he was still at school. When he went back and told his headmaster that he had been offered a job, he was advised to take it as "you are no use here". He began work at Gerrards in 1956 aged fourteen and a half. Don's first job was an egret, after which he became 'the bird person'. He did a lot of fish too, and this later became his main work. In 1957 he did a record pike for Colonel Atherstone and also set up scores of fox heads using the traditional methods based on wood wool and the original skull. He worked six days a week at College Place, travelling in from Luton each day to unlock the yard at about 7:30am before the others arrived, and leaving at 5.30 in the evening. In the winter months he stoked coke fires in three of the workrooms. Initially he was paid three pounds per week. Later he applied for a job with the prestigious firm of Rowland Ward Ltd, but was rejected at interview with the Director Gerald Best who feared that he would learn Ward's trade secrets and

return to Gerrards, who were seen as commercial competitors. Don Sharp finally left when Charles Gerrard retired and "taxidermy went right down". He declined a transfer to the Hire section and went to work at the Vauxhall car factory in Luton, before moving to the post of taxidermist at Wollaton Hall Museum, Nottingham in 1966.

Don became a founder member and staunch supporter of the Guild of Taxidermists, doing much to promote the acceptability of taxidermy at a time when it was regarded in a poor light. He was always full of eager enthusiasm for his work and would frequently give demonstrations at meetings of the Guild, mounting a bird or painting a fish, as everyone looked on, or creating amazingly realistic hollow wax fruit models while walking about describing the process. In his time he did almost every type of taxidermy from casting an adder to mounting a full sized zebra. Doubtless, the grounding at Gerrards made him such a successful and versatile taxidermist.

A year before he retired in 2003, I went to see him for a day. We sat in his workshop, surrounded by work in progress, teacups and a plaster death mask of himself made years ago. Throughout our talk, he was setting up a badger, wearing a tie and a nice shirt. There was no sign of a white coat even when a group of museum visitors was brought in. He then broke off manipulating the badger to talk about his fifty years experience as a taxidermist, explaining that he was pleased to preserve things forever rather than have them go to waste. Afterwards I asked why he was not forced to wear a white coat by the museum's safety officer, at least for appearances sake. He replied that white coats frightened the children, so staff were forbidden to wear them. This may have been true, but was just as likely an excuse to be more comfortable in his normal clothes.

He died in 2004, a sad loss to British taxidermy.

Don Sharp demonstrating to the Guild of Taxidermists how to make wax fruits and leaves.

Taxidermy Methods

Most of Gerrard's head and whole mounts were based on traditional 'bind-ups', made from wood wool (often called 'excelsior' by Americans). This was commonly used in those days as packing material for fragile items and fresh fruit. Fibrous masses of wood wool were bound tightly with twine around a framework of iron and wood to recreate the body of an animal before the skin was put in place over it. Bundles of wood wool were tied in place, roughly matching the shape of the animal's muscles.

Sometimes when the skin of a large animal was set in place on the artificial body there remained awkward areas where it hung in baggy folds due to it being too large for the bind-up's body shape. Rather than remove the skin and start again, the taxidermists would often use special 'stuffing irons' to thrust small bundles of wood wool into the cavities to fill them out. These tools were made from old screw drivers, with a notch filed into the squared off blade. This would gather the stuffing and carry it into place under the skin, but at the expense of making the finished animal look rather padded and rotund. This was a characteristic of many of Gerrard's mammals, especially in the early days. Later, with the advent of better methods and the use of papier maché manipulated under the skin, they were able to assert *"we do not STUFF animals. All our specimens are correctly modelled and where possible, the skin is soft dressed beforehand. Collectors are asked to send us all possible measurements, and not just the length of the head and body."*

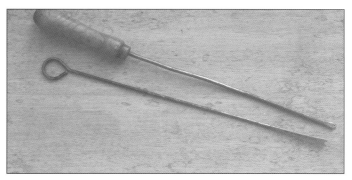

Stuffing irons were made from stiff wire or old screwdrivers, with a notch in the flat end.They were used to push stuffing into place under the skin and also to prise tail skin away from the bony core, by forcing the blade down below the skin itself.

The use of stuffing irons tended to result in very rotund animals, resembling upholstery rather than taxidermy. This is very evident in the overstuffed Dall sheep, photographed in Gerrard's yard.

Edward Gerrard Sr. had employed staff to twist hay into cords that could be rammed into larger specimens with 'stuffing irons'. A grainy photograph in the Daily Graphic (9 May 1914) shows the same method being used on a moose head.

Gerrard's tools

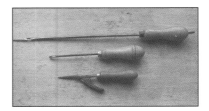

Various tools with eye and jaws for pushing threads through bind ups.

Very long needles were for making bind ups. When the rough shape of the body or a limb had been made, it was necessary to create hollows in places and to stop the whole shape from being too curvaceous. So tough yarn was passed through from one side to the other to pull in the surface and create flats or hollows. That was the function of the long needles- to reach right through the bind-up and out the other side. Twine used for binding up was wound on to a steel spindle so that a good grip could be maintained on it and the threads could be pulled tight.

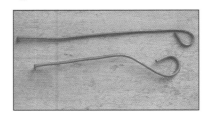

Brain scoops were for extracting brains from nooks and crannies within the cranium. They were made ad hoc from pieces of heavy gauge wire.

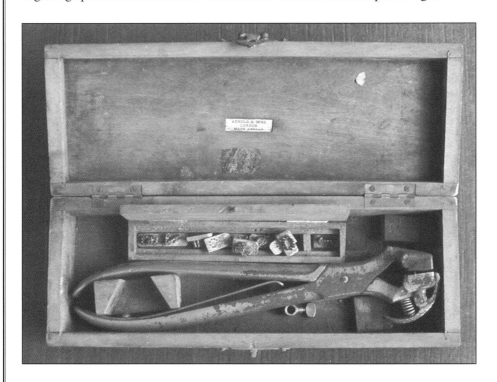

Envelopes full of whiskers were carefully kept for 'spares'.

Nailing pliers with serrated jaws used for pulling skins tight when nailing them out to dry.

Punch with adjustable numbers formed from batteries of sharp points, used to create an identifier number in skins before tanning.

Powder paints (right) were used to touch up bare skin, often mixed with a carrier such as wax, alcohol or shellac. In his book, Charles Gerrard noted "Water colours are not suitable being too thin. Even the driest and most non-greasy taxidermy specimens do not take kindly to water colours. Oil colours are excellent and should be used whenever possible. Powder paints are the most convenient if kept in a box with a well fitting lid and divided into compartments for the different colours. There will be little likelihood of the colours spilling. Powder colours may be mixed with methylated spirit on to a palette and for hardening, white polish should be used for the lighter colours and button or brown polish for the darker ones. Soft haired brushes are not suitable for powder painting and stiffer hair is called for and a supply of various sizes will be useful. Avoid black whenever possible as it is extremely light and liable to blow away".

Products and Customers

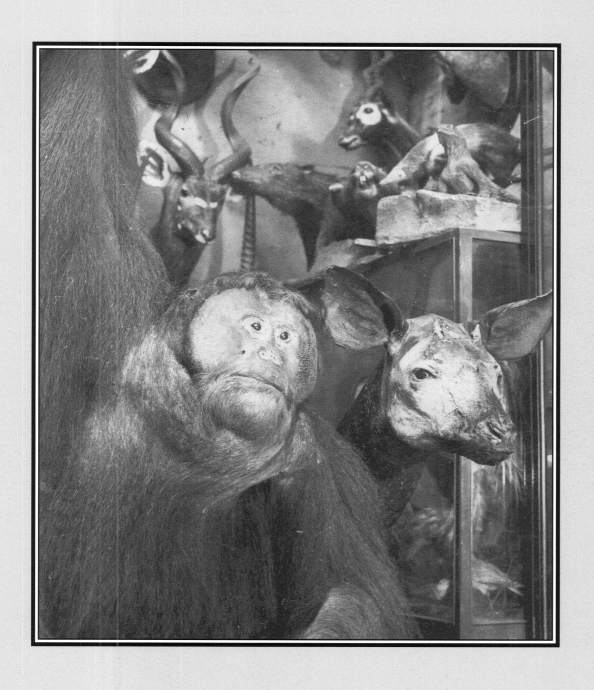

Chapter 4
Products and Customers

Gerrards advertised occasionally (in the London Zoo Visitors Guide for example) and periodically issued price lists and illustrated catalogues showing the wide range of work on offer. These and old photographs, dating from the early twentieth century, show that preparing game trophy heads, mostly from Africa, formed a major part of the business. Gerrards had a huge output of head mounts on their characteristic shields, and even today these are commonly seen in the antiques trade and in museums and large homes.

Clearly Gerrards were very productive in this area, servicing the big game hunters who had been collecting in various parts of the world, particularly in the Colonies.

Hunters made brief visits from Britain, but many also collected their trophies whilst on secondment to the Colonial administrations of Britain's former Empire.

Curiously, relatively few of the old photographs show tigers (or other distinctive Asian trophies), yet big game hunting was popular in Asia, especially India. Perhaps the market there was already well served by Rowland Ward Ltd of London, yet Wards were also well established in Africa and even opened a branch in Nairobi specifically to capture a larger share of the trophy trade. Despite this, Gerrards still managed to preserve a very large number of African specimens.

A selection of typical African trophy heads, dating from about 1907.

Perhaps Gerrards appealed to those who were unable to afford Ward's high charges? Yet, by contrast they appear to have done few similar specimens from Asia. Perhaps this was because they faced additional competition in India, where sportsmen also had available the services of many local taxidermists, foremost among them being Van Ingen and Van Ingen, 'Artists in Taxidermy' of Mysore. They produced extremely robust high quality trophies, using lightweight papier maché manikins that must have been attractive to those wishing to save on shipping costs. Moreover, trophies by Van Ingen could be ready and delivered to the customer in India within a few months, those sent to Gerrards in London were unlikely to be returned inside a year. So customers who lived in India would have little incentive to send their trophies back to Gerrards. This still does not explain the comparative lack of specimens and species from other parts of the Empire that were set up by Gerrards. The majority of their big game work consisted of African species.

Asian animals comparatively rarely figured among Gerrard's work, even tigers. African trophies, like the three quarters lion, (above) were much more common.

It is also curious that customers rarely made reference to their taxidermists in newspaper stories and books. For example, H.G. Mainwaring's book *'A Soldier's Shikar Trips'* includes long lists of safari kit needed, even down to the most trivial items, but no reference is made to the essential tools and materials required for skinning or preserving the trophies which were the main purpose of such expeditions. Moreover, Mainwaring's taxidermy was done by Gerrards, and his book illustrates many of their distinctive specimens, but there is no mention of that either, any more than he mentions his barber or cook.

Customers and suppliers

Animals were purchased from hunters or traded against the cost of preparing their own specimens. The explorer, Du Chaillu sent a gorilla in a rum cask and 'Trader Horn' also sent gorilla skulls and said Gerrards gave him a fair deal. Gerrards worked for many famous collectors and hunters, including Major P.H.G. Powell Cotton and his private museum in Kent. They also prepared many hunting trophies for Lord Kitchener, including forty bears made into a rug. Nevertheless, Gerrard's taxidermy was not confined to hunting trophies. In fact they prepared a remarkably wide range of species, and their 1951 price list even offered to mount a porpoise for £7/15/-.

Many taxidermists offered to visit private collections, like this one, to carry out installations and renovations. To what extent Gerrards did this too is not clear, but it was not prominent among their advertised services.

Some notable people associated with Gerrards

Lord Curzon, Viceroy of India

Lord Cromer (Bank of England)

Lord Kitchener,
Commander in Chief in World War I

Lord Baden Powell,
founder of the Boy Scouts

Lord Rothschild (said to have driven his team of zebras and cart to Gerrards from Piccadilly)

Sir Harry Johnstone,
European discoverer of the okapi

FC Selous,
hunter, traveller and author

The Maharajah of Gwalior,
famous Big Game hunter

The Sultan of Jahore and other Indian dignitories,
Various European and Egyptian princes

Trader Horne

Gerrards were unusual in supplying an extensive range of models, not just taxidermy. For example, they made models of villages depicting good and bad hygiene for the Uganda Medical Mission to "instruct the native population". Models were made of agricultural systems, showing good and bad fields, correct drainage systems, different types of fowl housing methods. There were also model mosquitoes, house flies and fleas to facilitate instruction in the threats that these creatures posed and the ways in which they could be controlled.

In addition to preparing trophies for hunters, Gerrards served many public museums, including those in Perth and Dublin, as well as London's Natural History Museum. Many overseas museums exhibited their work, including Moscow, Cairo, Bergen, Cleveland Ohio, New York, Ontario, Bulowayo, Durban and Sydney. Gerrards thus helped to establish many major institutions in the Empire and elsewhere. They seem to have done particularly well with Melbourne Museum. Pressed by the museum's energetic director, the first Edward Gerrard and his son supplied an elephant skeleton, a rhino head and a mounted hippo, along with deer, giraffes and sundry other large animals. The most famous items were three gorillas, originally collected by the adventurer Paul Du Chaillu and finally secured for the museum by Gerrards, four years after being asked to obtain some specimens.

They were originally preserved in salt, then mounted as a small family group among artificial rockwork and branches. On arrival in Australia in 1865 they fuelled an intense debate about human and primate evolution and doubled the number of visitors to the museum. They are still there, in the Museum Victoria, as examples of 19th century taxidermy with notable 'social history' connotations (Rasmusen, 2001).

Since Gerrards had easy access to dead animals produced by their close neighbour, the London Zoo, they were able to provide many rare specimens of zoological interest that were not readily available to museums from other sources. These could be purchased 'off the shelf' to extend a museum's own comprehensive collections and displays. Some of Gerrards more exotic species would have been bought as skins from collectors or at auctions, but most probably came from zoos, whose turnover of animals must have been very high in the days when major suppliers (like Carl Hagenbeck) maintained a steady flow of living curiosities. In days gone by, zoo keeping was less successful than now. Animals were considered expendable and easily replaced, so dead specimens were in constant supply.

Gerrard's staff frequently visited the nearby London Zoo to skin animals that had died recently. These included many common species such as camels and monkeys, but also rare species, including at least one of the Zoo's thylacines. Gerrards even mounted one of their precious quaggas (bought by Edinburgh Museum in 1879) and also sold its skeleton for £10, now in the Peabody Museum, Yale. (Edwards, 1996). Other bodies collected from the zoo included that of 'Brumas' the famous baby polar bear that had featured so prominently in newspapers, magazines and newsreel films. It was Don Sharp who went to the zoo with a two-wheeled handcart to spend all day skinning this popular and widely publicised animal and carry it back to the workshops, dripping blood through the streets as he went. Nobody noticed.

Prices for Gerrard's products

It seems that Gerrards issued very few price lists, and they are rarely seen today. Consequently, few costs have been available for analysis here. The three priced catalogues that I have been able to trace (in more than 20 years) do not cover the same items, restricting the comparisons that are possible. Moreover, they are not dated and I have relied on someone who added the date by hand when the lists were current.

A few more price lists were issued as single sheets or folded leaflets, probably in the 1940s and 1950s, but they are not dated and are therefore not referred to here. As prices steadily increased over the decades, lists are meaningless without an indication of date. In any case, prices given for preparation of customers own specimens were always only for guidance, with the emphasis being on seeing the specimen first.

As an alternative to issuing a long series of price lists, Gerrards often quoted for individual jobs instead. This would also help overcome the problem that their jobs were so varied that any list was almost bound to be incomplete and only any use for the most general guidance. A letter dated 1898 quoted £120 to build a model of half a humpbacked whale to fit the skeleton already in the Dublin Museum. Another letter in 1901 offered a badger skeleton (for £1-15/-), and one the following year offered to supply Dublin with a stuffed elephant shrew for 50/-. Similar hand written letters signed "Edwd Gerrard" appear in several archives, with the first typewritten examples dating from 1913.

Some notable animals prepared by Gerrards

(from a list compiled by Gerrards in the 1960s)

Moina,
a famous gorilla

Sam & Barbara,
two polar bears done for Madame Tussauds

Mickey the chimpanzee from Liverpool Zoo,
figured in *'The Naked Ape'* by Desmond Morris.

Hector,
a bear that lived in London Zoo for 28 years

A reconstruction of a giant armadillo from South America, as big as a mini car

The largest adult orang-utan to reach Britain alive from the Far East..

Elephants, whales, giraffes and okapi.

A basking shark featured in the film 'Man of Arran'.

Prices changed with time

Gerrard's price lists also show the effects of inflation and rising costs, even in pre-war years. Although the rate of inflation was nothing like as high as in the 1970s, when it reached about 15% per year, prices did change nevertheless, and lists were likely to have become obsolete quite quickly.

	1921	1932
Sunshade	25/-	25/-
Dog whip	10/6d	21/-
Small Paper knife	4/-	6/-
Riding switch	10/6d	15/-

A note about prices as given in this book

Prices given here are in 'old money', i.e. in pounds (£) shillings (/-) and pence (d), written as £x/x/x/. There were twelve pence to the shilling and twenty shillings to the pound. Although ten shillings (10/-) is therefore half of a pound, like 50p today, it is virtually impossible to translate these old prices to present day values. A better sense of scale is gained by relating prices to contemporary wages or costs of everyday items at a similar period. The table below may help set in context the prices given in this book (based on Priestly, 1979).

Date	Bread – 4lb loaf	Eggs- per dozen	Sugar- per pound	Typical house	Skilled male weekly wage	Unskilled
	prices in old pence (d)					
1921-30	3½ d	11d	2½d	£600	£5	£4
1931-40	4d	7½d	1d	£750	£5	£4
1951-60	10½d	1/11d	1d	£2,750	£11	£7

Heads

Chapter 5
Heads

The most numerous of Gerrard's taxidermy products were antelope head mounts. They probably prepared thousands of these, often in large batches as customers shipped home crates of specimens obtained on big game hunts lasting weeks and months. The specimens were skinned in the field, often by skilled local men. The skins (or scalps in the case of head trophies) were then salted or dried before being crated for shipment home. The skull was roughly dried or cleaned up by boiling or maceration, but Gerrards specifically advised their customers to send skins and skulls separately. This was to avoid the danger of insect pests in the latter infesting the precious skins and causing irreparable damage to them on the long voyage to England.

Gerrard's trophy heads were usually mounted on a distinctive 'U'- shaped shield, with the top corners scooped out. These highly characteristic mounts are common in collections and mostly have withstood the passage of time quite well. The characteristic shields were in use at least from about 1905, and remained unchanged for over 50 years. They are very evident in photographs and in collections and enable Gerrard's work to be easily recognised without the need to lift the specimen down from the wall to look for a label on the back. Sometimes other shield shapes were used, at the request of customers. The wood was usually 'fumed oak', although other hardwoods were available. Trophies were also supplied without shields, reducing the cost.

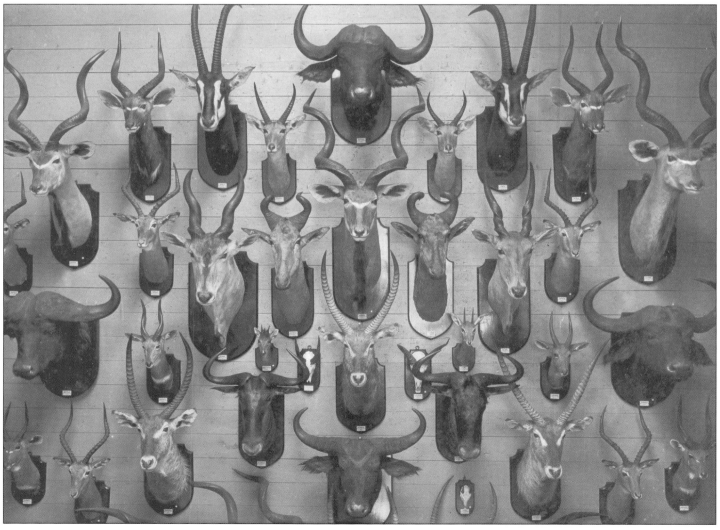

Heads were often sent to Gerrards in large batches, following a successful hunting trip abroad. They were then usually mounted on a distinctive 'U' shaped shield, with the top corners scooped out.

Shields

Like Rowland Ward Ltd and several other leading taxidermists, Gerrards used a standard and distinctive shape for the wooden shield on which their trophy heads were mounted. Gerrard's characteristic shields were 'U' shaped, with the top corners cut out as semicircular notches. The sides of the shield were not bevelled. These characteristic shields were in use for head mounts at least as early as 1905 and continued unchanged well into the 1960s. Making them was contracted out to another supplier, who usually cut them from planks of heavy

A youthful Charles Gerrard holds up a stag head mount for the camera.

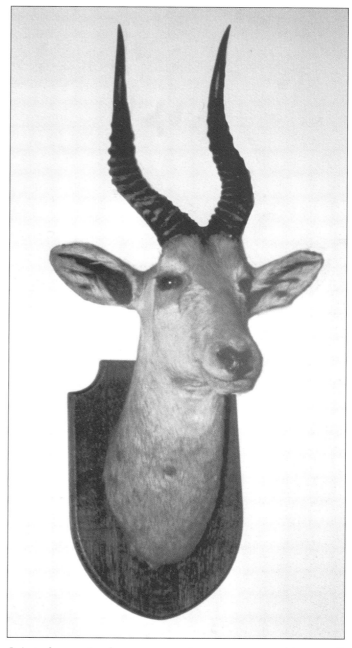

Bill Dwyer (one of Gerrard's employees who habitually wore a trilby hat to work), with blank shields for fox masks.

It is truly amazing how many specimens were created in a small yard in Camden Town, and how far across the world they subsequently travelled. This head mount was photographed in Pretoria, having been shot in Africa, sent to London to be mounted and then returned for display.

oak, but other woods were available on request. In his unpublished book, Charles Gerrard commented that it was "a good idea to make your own pattern and keep to one style as a kind of trademark" and that "the manufacture of these is really the job of a cabinet maker and not the taxidermist, but it is very satisfying to carry on a job right through from beginning to end and it is a lot cheaper too".

The shields often bore labels on the front to say when and where the animal was shot. Labels were available in ivorine (made from a type of white plastic resembling ivory) and Gerrard's offered a wide range of different styles, as shown opposite. Ivorine labels sometimes had their lettering added to the surface, but this easily wore off. Letters engraved into the plastic were more durable and permanent, but also more expensive. Relatively few Gerrard shields carry ivorine labels. Instead, the information was often painted directly on to the wood by hand. Perhaps the use of hand painted lettering was cheaper and helped to reduce the total price of the job. This would be consistent with the fact that Rowland Ward Ltd had a reputation for the highest quality and attracted the richest and most prominent clientele, leaving the lesser, more cost conscious, customers to deal with Gerrards.

Two characteristic shield designs - Gerrards (left) and Rowland Ward (right).

Prices of Mammal head mount trophies

In 1921, skulls on shields were priced from about 8/- (fox) to 20/- (buffalo, tiger), with big hippos and rhinos costing up to 50/-. Prices were always quoted for looking straight ahead, there was an extra charge for turning to one side or other poses. Frontlets (horns with the top of the skull linking them) were 6/- to 9/- in 1921, but had increased to £3/10/- by 1951. At that time, lion and tiger heads cost an extra £2 for mounting with the mouth open, showing the modelled tongue. This represents over 20% more for a mouth-open trophy, a reflection of the considerable extra work involved.

Most of Gerrard's trophy head mounts were of antelopes.

Engraved ivorine labels cost 1/- to 2/6d in 1921, depending on size, but relatively few Gerrard head mounts have ivorine data labels. It was more common on Gerrard shields to have information about where and when the trophy was obtained written directly on to the wood by hand in white or gold letters. This was charged at 1/4d per dozen letters. In practice, there was probably little difference in cost for a typical data label done this way as against using ivorine, but cheaper still was to have no label at all, and that is the case with the majority of Gerrard heads.

Glass eyes were bought for use in the workshops and were also offered for sale by the dozen. In 1951, eyes 15mm in diameter were 7/10d per dozen, a similar number of 36mm eyes cost 55/-. Plain black eyes were cheaper.

Normal glass eyes had a simple black pupil and a coloured surround (iris), rather like teddy bears eyes, and many of Gerrard's early heads have these, even though certain species do not have such a simple ocular anatomy. The eye of a reindeer or ibex for example, requires an oblong pupil, unavailable in those days from suppliers of enamelled glass eyes. These special eyes could be created by hand-painting the inside of a plain glass cup. Gerrards had a large stock of these glass 'blanks' to colour as needed. They would also supply painted eyes to customers or other taxidermists. They cost 50% more than standard glass eyes and were much better (but they were only available on sizes of 15mm and above).

Above: Two pages of suggestions for label designs.

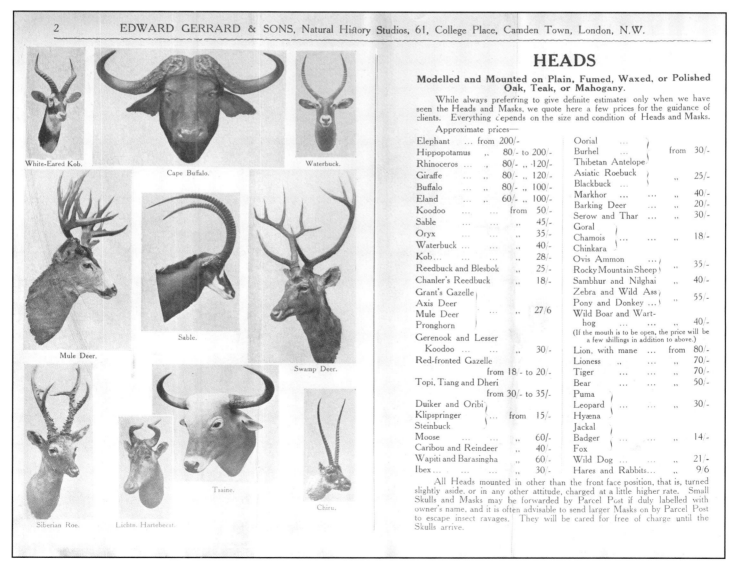

Pages from a Gerrard catalogue, showing prices of head mounts in 1921, with some typical examples.

Table of head mount costs

On plain, fumed, waxed or polished oak, teak or mahogany shield. Guide prices were given in £, the actual price charged would depend on the condition of the specimen.

Species	1921	1951
Elephant	£10+	–
Hippo	£4-£10	–
Rhino, giraffe	£4-£6	£10
Buffalo	£4-£5	£9/10/-
Eland, kudu	£3-£5	£4-15/-
Moose	£3	£8/10/-
Duiker, steinbok	From 15/-	£2/10/-
Tiger, mouth shut	£3/10/-	£9
Leopard	£1/10/-	£6
Fox, badger	14/-	£2/10/
Small gazelles, etc	£1-15/-	£3-15/
Hares, rabbit	9/6d	–

A Rocky Mountain goat shot in 1931 and set up by Gerrards on a polished oval shield, a departure from their normal style.

Throughout Gerrard's time in business otters and badgers were legal quarry and large numbers of them were killed and set up as trophy mounts.

Occasionally there was improvisation, and I once saw a Gerrard nilghai head like this whose eyes were made from the curved glass lumps broken out from the base of two wine bottles.

A selection of trophy heads

These two were prepared in 1956 (left) and 1931 (right), both by the traditional method of arranging the skin over stuffing built up around the actual skull.

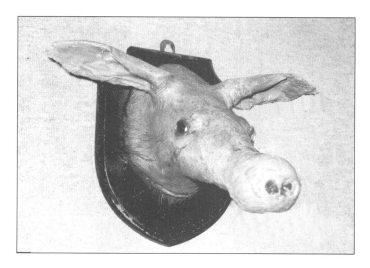

Gerrard's prepared very few tiger heads, despite the numbers of these animals that were shot by hunters in India.

Whoever bagged the warthog (below) was no doubt proud of it as a trophy, but who on earth wanted a head mount of an aardvark?

Each year, from August onwards, fox heads would arrive, usually through the post. They were a regular job for Gerrard's just as for most other taxidermists.

A selection of trophy head collections

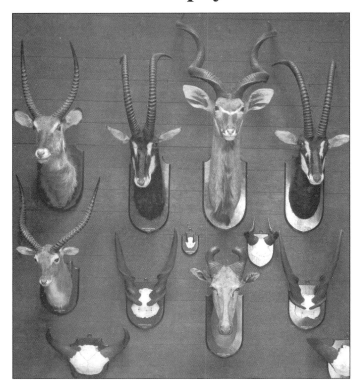 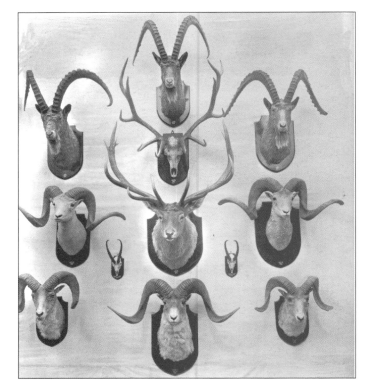

The Rogue Elephant

 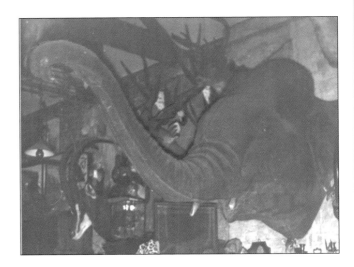

For many years, this elephant head hung in Gerrard's showroom, surrounded by all kinds of other things. Later it stood in a corner of the Hire Company's store. Its appearance was distinctive as was the story of its acquisition.

According to legend, repeated in the 'Evening Standard' of 11th October 1938, this animal was running amok in Ceylon (now Sri Lanka), causing untold mischief among the local villages. Four English sportsmen resolved to kill it, but although they did succeed, it was only after a very dangerous encounter that nearly cost them their lives. They had the head preserved and every year, at the Kensington home of the man who fired the fatal shot, they met to celebrate the event. The dinner table was set against the wall under the elephant's head, and after the meal the men

would rise to their feet and toast their victim. After the last member of the team died, the preserved elephant's head was passed to Gerrards, where it remained for years as a prominent item in the showroom, visible in many of the contemporary photographs. It was later transferred to the Hire Company, where it stood upright in a corner and rarely left the store, being hemmed in by a large refrigerator. Moreover, it weighed 8.5 hundredweight (430kg) and required the combined efforts of several men to move it.

The head was included in the collection of animals bought for Potter's Museum in Cornwall in 1991 when the Hire Company was closing down. Press photographs show it being installed in the upper part of the museum using a crane. There it hung in the roof, suspended above an

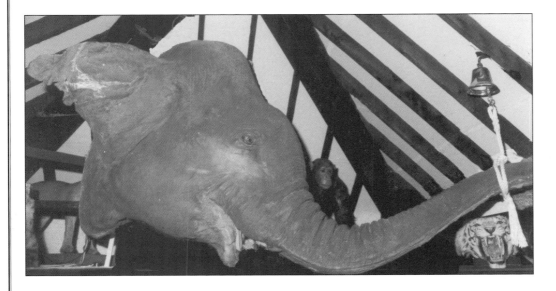

upstairs doorway, as though tugging at a small brass bell that served to hide the wires that prevented the head from swaying about. It was sold for £3,000 at the auction of Potters Museum in September 2003, with the new owner demanding to know why a crane was not available late in the afternoon to retrieve it from the roof out on the wilds of Bodmin Moor.

Whole Mount Mammals

Chapter 6
Whole Mount Mammals

Gerrards created considerable numbers of mammal whole mounts, both large and small, for collectors and museums. They included cows, rhinos, giraffes and at least one famous hippopotamus. Because of their size, the largest mammals were a particular challenge to taxidermists and few ever managed to prepare adult examples, especially elephants. Such jobs required a small team of men, because of the sheer weight of the skin and materials needing to be manipulated.

Nevertheless, despite the limitations on space and manpower, Gerrards mounted several elephants, although some were only small ones. One Indian elephant, nearly 2m (6 ft) high, was prepared for the Blackpool fun fair. It comprised 12ft of planks and 15ft of two-inch wire mesh, covered with canvas and a layer of papier maché below the skin. It took 18 months to dry. Another elephant was 'Lizzie', a circus animal that died in 1888 in Wales. The body was sold to Swansea Museum for £20 and Edward Gerrard was summoned from London to supervise its preservation for a fee of £40, plus £8/15/3d expenses. Lizzie stood in the entrance hall of the museum for 60 years, a delight to visitors, many of whom climbed on her back or stroked her from the staircase. She deteriorated sufficiently that she was dismantled and burnt in the early 1950s.

The largest of Gerrard's elephants was probably "Jung Pasha", one of four brought back from Asia for the London Zoo by Bertie the Prince of Wales (the future King Edward Vllth) following his tour of India in 1875-76. The animal was only about five years old at the time, but spent twenty further years in Regents Park, where he was popular among the thousands of children who were given rides on his back. He died from peritonitis in March 1896, and was mounted by Gerrards for display in the central hall of the Natural History Museum.

Some noteworthy zoo mammals

The quagga is a form of zebra, now extinct, that used to roam the plains of South Africa in large herds. London Zoo exhibited three of them in the mid-nineteenth century. The first was acquired in November 1831 and is probably the mounted specimen on display at the Natural History Museum in London. It was prepared by Gerrard's, but at some later stage (perhaps as a result of the dryness associated with the generous heating in public institutions) the skin split badly and the relatively crude repairs remain visible to this day. Gerrards also mounted the Zoo's second quagga, which died in 1872, after more than 20 years on display. This one is now at

A selection of large mammals by Gerrards

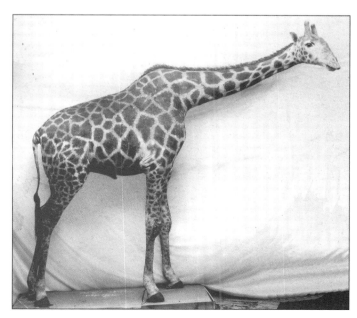

the National Museums of Scotland in Edinburgh, having been purchased from Gerrards in 1879. Gerrards also mounted her skeleton and sold it o the Peabody Museum at Yale University in 1873 for just £10 (Edwards, 1996).

Sam the polar bear was another famous London Zoo inhabitant who subsequently passed through Gerrards workshops. Sam and his mate Barbara first lived in some sterile concrete enclosures, but were later transferred to the new Mappin Terraces, the first polar bears to live there. It is said that one of them bit the padlock off the gate and the pair wandered freely around the zoo. The two bears were popular with the public and were often mentioned in the Press. They produced several families of cubs, although none survived. Sam was purchased in 1903 and put down in 1923. (Edwards, 1996). A contemporary newspaper photograph shows Jim Scuds and Charles Gerrard working on Sam's skin prior to mounting. Other notable zoo mounts included several giant tortoises done by Gerrards for Lord Rothschild.

Ming was one of five pandas collected by Mr Floyd Smith in 1938 in western China. They were brought to England and started a hug craze for cuddly toys and everything panda or black and white. Three of these valuable animals were retained by the London Zoo, of which Ming was the last survivor. She was a great favourite in the Children's Zoo, and attracted many thousands of additional visitors to Regents Park. In fact she was probably the most famous and popular of all the zoo's exhibits. Ming was evacuated to Whipsnade during the War, but returned to London several times in

Mickey the chimpanzee was reputed to have come originally from Blackpool Tower Circus. He later served many years with Gerrard Hire Ltd. A picture of him alive appeared on the dustjacket of the controversial book 'The Naked Ape' by Desmond Morris.

spite of the blitz. After a brief illness, she died in her sleep at the Zoo on Christmas Day 1944.

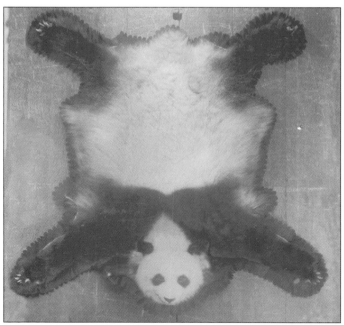

Ming in Gerrard's showroom (right) and her skin (left) nailed to a board at an earlier stage of preparation.

Specimens brought in by customers could be skinned on the spot, but Gerrards would also mount mammals from dried skins sent by post, although in that case the lower leg bones were also requested in order to establish the correct body proportions. In addition, the taxidermists worked on animals obtained from collectors and zoos, creating specimens as speculative sales and offering them as being immediately available ('off the shelf').

EST. 1850   EUSton 2765

EDW. GERRARD & SONS

Taxidermists, Modellers, Furriers, etc.

61 College Place, Camden Town

LONDON, N.W.1

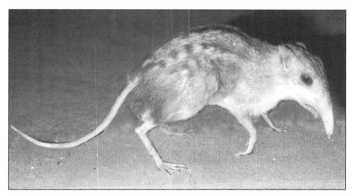

An elephant shrew with its label (above) and an x-ray of the mounted specimen. Smaller mammals like this were supported on a wire framework, made by pushing wires up through the legs and twisting them together inside the skin. The limb bones were left in place in this animal, perhaps to help retain the correct stance and leg proportions. Soft stuffing was then loosely pushed in to fill out the skin. The skull remains in place, with the back of the cranium cut away to remove the brain. Clay has been added around the anterior part of the skull to provide a smooth finish to the snout, which would otherwise have shrivelled and lost its natural appearance. The glass eyes were set in clay, forming two x-ray opaque blobs on the front of the head. The right forefoot is raised so its wire is not anchored to the base.

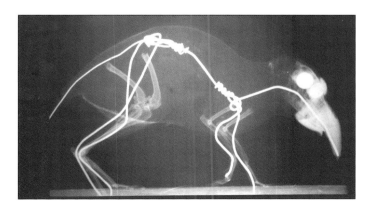

This would have been especially attractive to schools and museums wanting particular species now, rather than having to wait until a suitable corpse was found. A comparison of prices in 1951 of whole mounts bought off the shelf and those mounted from customers own skins or carcasses, shows that storage costs and the risk of not selling it meant that a ready-made specimen cost more. A ready-mounted fox cost about one third more than mounting a customer's own animal, but the much rarer wild cat cost three times as much as a cat brought in to be mounted. So scarcity affected the price too. For example, an available dormouse cost five times as much as one brought in by a customer. It was also three times as much as an ordinary mouse off the shelf, although the work needed to prepare them was the same, an indication of the rarity value of a dormouse. Similarly, a

Prices in 1951

Whole mounts immediately available compared to the cost of mounting similar animals brought in by the customer, either as a fresh body or as suitably dried skin (in the latter case with the skull and leg bones).

Species	Ready mounted	Mounting customer's own
Mice	18/6	15/-
Dormouse	£3/15/-	15/-
Badger	£8/15/-	£5/10/-
Bat	£1/18/6d	£1/12/6
Fox	£8/0/0	£5/10/-
Hedgehog	£2/10/-	£1/10/-
Mole	£1/15/-	£1/15/-
Otter	£8/10/-	£5/10/-
Rabbit	£1/15/-	£1/17/6d
Stoat	£1/17/6d	£1/5/-
Wild cat	£15/0/0	£5/0/0

black rat was £1/17/6d, 23% (7/-) more than a common brown rat and a red squirrel cost £2/15, 18% (10/-) more than a grey.

Like most other taxidermists, Gerrards regularly prepared trophies during the fox and otter hunting season (otter hunting was still legal and widespread until the mid 1960s). The trophies comprised heads, tails and feet. The latter cost about £2-£3, among the least expensive items on offer.

<table>
<tr><td colspan="2">Some prices in 1951</td></tr>
<tr><td colspan="2">For mounting whole foreign mammals, from customers' own specimens, with skull and limb bones also present.</td></tr>
<tr><td>Leopard, wolf, gazelle</td><td>£7/15/-</td></tr>
<tr><td>Chimpanzee, porpoise, wallaby</td><td>£7/15/-</td></tr>
<tr><td>Sheep, Shetland pony</td><td>£10/10/-</td></tr>
<tr><td>Tapir, lesser kudu</td><td>£17/10/-</td></tr>
<tr><td>Lion, tiger, reindeer</td><td>£35</td></tr>
<tr><td>Sea lion, hartebeest</td><td>£35</td></tr>
<tr><td>Horse, zebra, polar bear</td><td>From £100</td></tr>
<tr><td>Elephant, rhino, hippo</td><td>From £125</td></tr>
<tr><td>Giraffe</td><td>£150</td></tr>
</table>

An otter foot hunting trophy on a typical small Gerrard shield. There were still 13 Otter Hunts active in England and Wales in the 1950s and otter hunting remained legal until 1978. Although hunting success declined, each pack of otter hounds hunted for about 40-50 days per year and killed 15-20 otters annually. The paws of otters, foxes and badgers were preserved by turning the skin inside out to the finger tips, then usually the bones were removed and replaced by clay, modelled into shape through the skin. If the skin and flesh were simply allowed to dry on the bone, the toes would shrivel and be liable to breakage. The foot would also then be vulnerable to attack by carnivorous insects.

An astonished kinkajou!

Habitat groups

Habitat groups, like those shown here, were often assembled in Gerrard's yard, before they were transported to a museum for installation on site.

Some lions and orang-utans

Some smaller species

These included a lot of rare and obscure animals (such as the otter shrew, hammer headed fruit bat and striped weasel seen here) that were probably not collected in the field for taxidermy. They are more likely to have been obtained alive for zoos, then sold to Gerrards when they died. Mounted specimens would have been attractive to museums and teaching institutions, unable to obtain such curiosities by other means.

Huberta the famous hippo

In November 1928, this hippo embarked upon one of the strangest journeys ever undertaken by a large mammal. It left the muddy pools of Zululand and headed south to become one of Africa's most famous travellers. Within days there were reports of a hippo wandering down the coast and soon she was found munching her way into a sugar cane plantation. A press report about this incident, named the animal 'Hubert the Hippo' as the culprit, only later was it discovered that the animal was a female and required renaming. For a while she lived in a pool near the railway. Trains would slow down to allow passengers to see her and throw fruit to eat. Local bus trips offered to take tourists on visits.

Over the next three years, Huberta ambled some 1,600km through South Africa, crossing roads, railway tracks, fields and a golf course. She ate her way through crops and gardens, even wandering into the outskirts of towns. Her epic travels were followed by the press and public. Meanwhile, Johannesburg Zoo decided to try and capture her, and an expedition set off with a newsreel crew. Huberta made a run for it, with catchers and newsmen in hot pursuit. It all made good stories, popular with the public, and after a while the local government afforded her full legal protection (as 'Royal game') and the zoo had to give up its chase, empty-handed. One night a truck driver found her asleep under a bridge near Durban and nudged her off the road with his bumper. She ran away and hid, but soon all Durban was keen to see her. She spent the summer holiday season in a nearby lagoon, off the Durban beach, being fed regularly by well wishers and bathing in the sea. In March she set off again and her footprints were seen on a local golf course, then in a housing estate. This gave rise to a story that she was looking for a house but couldn't find

one with a big enough bathroom. One night in April she gate crashed a party at the Durban Country Club, causing consternation and she ended up entering the city itself, where in the early morning she was seen at a Chemist's shop and later plodding through the streets to a nearby river. She continued her wanderings, passing further down the coast of Natal, feted by the local people. During her travels, she was deified by Hindus and various native peoples apparently believed her to be the reincarnation of famous witch doctors and other traditional notables. Near East London, she was found asleep on the railway track and a train driver had to nudge her off the rails to pass by safely.

Her luck ran out in April 1931 when she was found floating in the Keiskamma River, apparently having been shot. Parliament discussed the heinous crime and the police arrested four local farmers. They were each fined £25 for killing Royal Game, Huberta's bullet-ridden skull forming a gruesome and smelly court exhibit. The body had been recovered by the Director of the Kaffrerian Museum in King Williams Town, who took a taxi to the scene of the crime and arranged for some locals to help with skinning the rapidly deteriorating carcass. He took the skin and skull back to the museum by bus, where floral tributes and inquisitive visitors poured in. He sent the skin to London to be mounted by Edward Gerrard & Sons. The total cost (including transport back on the SS City of Hong Kong) was £159-19-6d., raised by public appeals. The animal was proudly displayed in the Museum as a national heroine, and later attracted over 20,000 visitors when on loan to the Durban museum for a mere five weeks. She subsequently inspired countless paintings and poems and even pieces of music.

Domestic dogs

Pet dogs and cats became a speciality with Gerrards. Many taxidermists would not touch them for a variety of reasons, including the fact that they were often very fat and difficult to preserve properly, but Gerrards mounted considerable numbers and did them well, including 'Susan', the Yorkshire terrier shown here (below), prepared in 1956. Dogs or cats purchased as finished mounts cost upwards of £6/10/- but only £5 if customers brought their own animal in to be preserved.

Mick the Miller

Mick and his chauffeur-driven car.

When he died in 1938, his body was presented to the Natural History Museum and arrangements were made for him to be prepared by Charles Gerrard. Mick is now exhibited among the famous mounted dog collection at the Rothschild Zoological Museum, Tring. The mounted animal serves as a permanent memorial to a memorable dog, whose speed and clever tactics brought major cash benefits to many people from all walks of life. He also provides an example of the finest quality taxidermy associated with Gerrards.

Mick was the most famous greyhound of the twentieth century and one of the best-known of all Gerrard's work. He was born in 1926 in Ireland and brought to England where he immediately began to win races at the White City greyhound track. He was then sold for £800 and went on to win further major races, increasing his value such that he was later sold again for £2000. By 1931 he had contested 48 races and won 36 of them, including four Classics. Mick was famous and pampered, even being driven about by a chauffeur in a limousine. He brought riches to his owners and backers alike, and his talents were perpetuated by spending his last few years at stud.

Charles Gerrard working on Mick, following the original measurements record (right)

Animal Furniture

Chapter 7
Animal Furniture, Rugs etc.

Although we find it strange, and even offensive, to think of animals being made into furniture, it was not always so. Indeed it was viewed as an interesting and ingenious way of putting to use what might otherwise be wasted. After all, if elephants were being shot in large numbers for their ivory, it was a pity to waste the feet, ears and other bits of their anatomy that could be made into functional household items. Moreover, these might also serve as souvenirs of a memorable hunting trip, or simply a novel and interesting type of furniture.

Rowland Ward Ltd offered a lot of this type of taxidermy as a speciality. So did Gerrards. Keen to sell similar things, but at lower prices, they illustrated a vast assortment of different designs in their brochures, ranging from zebra skin screens to doorstops made from rhino feet. This type of product would be made up from a customer's own skins, which had to be in good condition.

The fabrication of household furniture from parts of animals, including waste bins made from elephant feet, lamps from the feet of rhinos and hippos, and tables supported on straightened zebra legs, became a classic Gerrard speciality. These items were a major and evidently popular line of work in the 1920s and 1930s, as shown by their dominance in contemporary Gerrard catalogues. An elephant foot containing cut glass

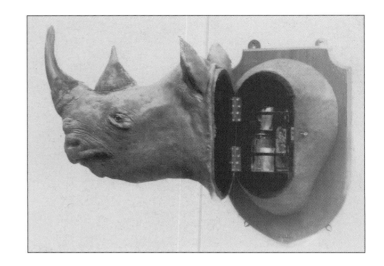

decanters cost 90/- in 1921. My favourite is a drinks cabinet inside the head of a rhinoceros, no doubt created to grace an imposing household. Few things could more graphically illustrate the change in attitudes towards animals that took place during the past century

A selection of these items is shown on the following pages, including some of the artwork prepared for use in sales brochures. The photographs are mostly from Gerrard's own albums that were shown to customers to indicate what might be made available.

Animal skins could easily be substituted for plain leather to make unusual armchairs and other household furniture, featuring the natural patterns of hair and fur. Gerrards also supplied tables, cabinets, chairs and other furniture, in which some of the wooden panels were replaced by sheets of specially treated skin from crocodiles or large mammals such as elephants or rhinos (whose skin is about 1cm thick, dries hard as a sheet of plywood and could take a fine polish).

Rhino hide could also be fashioned into dog whips, walking sticks and umbrella handles (all costing about £1 each), or turned like wood to make chessmen or

small bowls. Animal furniture was expensive. Hide topped tables cost about £6-£8 in 1921, the most expensive being a rhino hide and mahogany table standing on legs made from impala horns. An ostrich egg sweet dish to stand on it was also available (but cost extra). In 1932, a normal height table, topped with rhino or elephant hide cost the equivalent of two weeks wages for an average skilled worker like a policeman.

These small free-standing screens cost about 63/- to 75/-. Simple hand held screens containing only the wings or breast of a bird set on an ebonised handle cost from 15/6d in 1932.

Gerrards also made a number of 'dumb waiters' consisting of an upright bear holding a small tray. These were very popular at one time and are still frequently seen in the antiques trade. Probably less appealing were the large pythons, formed into standard lamps by being

Other types of table were supported on animal legs, specially stretched and straightened to gain sufficient height. The lanky zebra legs are disturbing enough, but the fact that the table legs all faced different directions also looks distinctly odd.

Large screens were offered in which panels of skin were stretched on frames. This was a good way of using the visually arresting skins of zebras. Their hair is brittle and zebra skins that are made into floor coverings soon become bald with use, due to people walking over them.

Smaller, lightweight screens were made to hide fireplaces. Often these were in the form of a tall wooden stand, supporting a narrow glass case. This might contain a group of colourful birds or butterflies, or sometimes a single spreadeagled individual bird.

wrapped around a tree stump and equipped with a light fitting. Not only are snakes widely reviled, but they are difficult to mount without their long axis becoming twisted unnaturally. The scales often lift too, becoming ragged as they dry, creating a very nasty object.

It seems that almost anything could be made to order, allowing the customer's own ingenuity to be used creatively. And there seemed to be no lack of imagination. One woman wanted a whole crocodile mounted as a couch for ladies to sit on at her tea parties, like the fireside fender mounted on rhino feet, shown here.

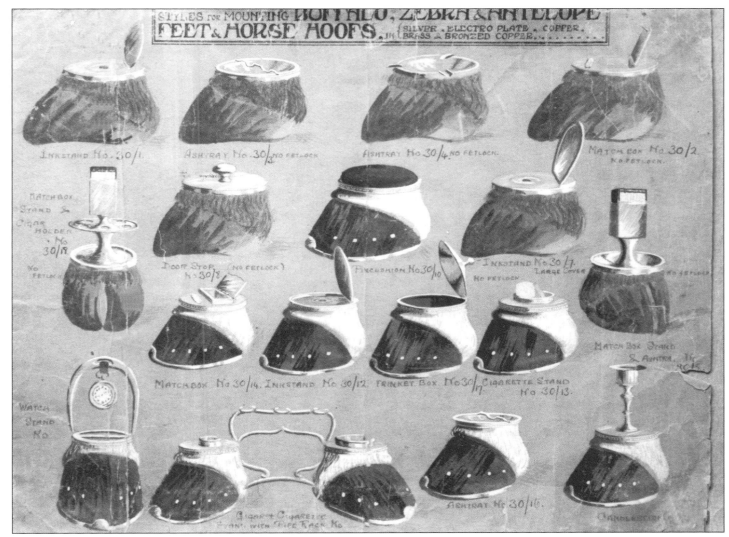

Some of Gerrard's original artwork, possibly done by Charles Gerrard, who was a capable artist. This panel illustrates a selection of items made from horses' hooves. In his own book, Charles Gerrard described the preparation of hooves as "the most frustrating job one can have in taxidermy. I do not like the work involved. My arms, hands and fingers ache at the thought of the strain required to force the bone out of the hoof". The metal fittings were of brass, copper or electro-plated silver. They were evidently made elsewhere, probably by the same metalworkers that supplied other taxidermists. In fact, these items were almost identical to those offered by Rowland Ward Ltd, despite the latter's assertion that the designs were patented. Perhaps Ward's patents had expired, leaving Gerrards (and others) free to produce similar items.

Tusks

Elephant tusks were usually mounted separately in their natural state, each standing upright from a circular wooden base. However, the tusks of warthogs and especially hippos were made into a much wider range of ingenious products. Mostly the tusks were used to frame mirrors or dinner gongs, like those here made in the 1920s, but they could also be employed to support lamps, candle sticks and clocks or they could be turned into paper knives and bottle openers. The illustrations on this page show artwork advertising tusk-based products, together with some actual examples.

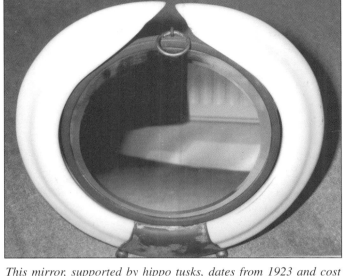

This mirror, supported by hippo tusks, dates from 1923 and cost about 55/-

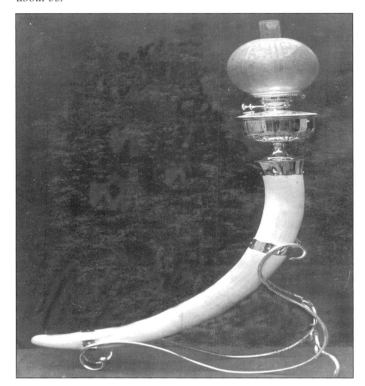

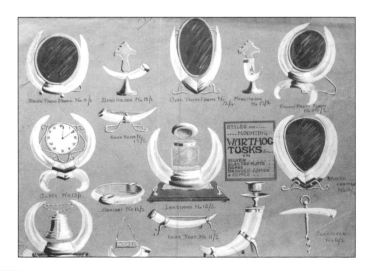

Rugs and skins

In the post-war years especially, rugs were a speciality of Gerrards, both for laying on the floor and as wall hangings. The rug making business was very successful and many are still seen today.

Skins were sent to a tannery and then, back at College Place, they were cut to shape, lined with canvas and trimmed with coloured felt. This was usually crimped (bunched into folds along the edge) using a special type of sewing machine. Customers could choose how their rug was made up and the choice would be affected by the condition of the skin and by its species. Deer and other ungulates would normally have the legs cut short and the head removed, but bears, tigers and leopards often had the head raised and padded. Better still (but about 20% more expensive) was to have was to have the head fully modelled. The mouth could be open or closed, depending on cost and skin condition.

In the case of large predators such as lions and tigers, the heads were sometimes modelled on papier maché head forms supplied by the Van Ingen factory in southern India. The forms were made in special moulds as part of Van Ingen's own taxidermy business.

Rugs left on the floor in customer's houses usually became severely damaged by people's feet and also during normal housework. Heads often lost whiskers and teeth as a result. Gerrards kept a large store of both

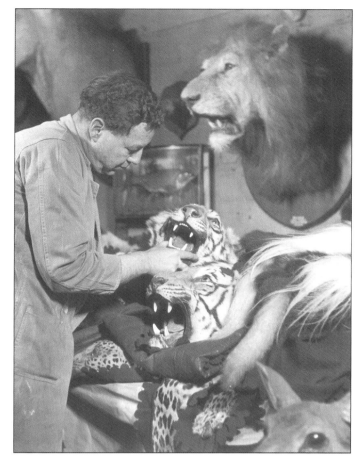

Charles Gerrard checking on some rugs in the showroom in 1947. Apart from the two tigers with modelled heads, a leopard rug is partially visible, edged with coloured felt, and also the long white hairs of a colobus monkey rug. Other contemporary photographs show that this heap also included four lion skins.   © *Mirrorpix*

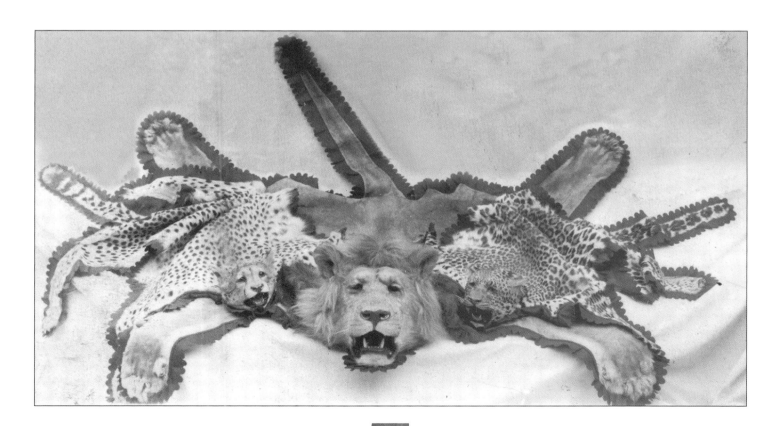

in order to provide replacements as necessary. Whiskers were also liable to be stolen (especially from tigers) by local people long before the skins got home, so substitutes would be needed back at the workshop, especially for preparing trophy heads, where the absence of whiskers or teeth would seriously detract from the appearance of the mount. Spare whiskers were obtained from skins sent to the tannery, but which were unusable for various reasons (torn or decayed for example). The taxidermists would salvage whatever they could from these reject skins, especially the whiskers. Spare bits of skin were also saved to patch good specimens. Gerrards had a large store of skin pieces which were especially useful to the Hire Company for repairing specimens damaged while out on loan to careless borrowers.

Tanned skins could also be 'dressed' (thinned down and softened with special vegetable oils) then made into clothing or used as blankets. Dressing skins was a specialist task and Gerrards sent their skins to J A Fisher & Co. Flat skins, backed and felt trimmed cost upwards of £3.

After tanning and dressing, a selection of skins could each be trimmed to a rectangular shape and sewn together to make a large carriage rug (used like a blanket to keep the knees warm in an open topped car or horse drawn carriage). A carriage rug 6ft x 5ft (1.8m x 1.5m) would need 18-20 cat size skins, and such rugs were often made up from wildcats trapped by gamekeepers.

A combination of Gerrard products from 1921- a chair with crocodile skin back standing on a tiger skin rug.

A bear skin rug with modelled head and mouth open.

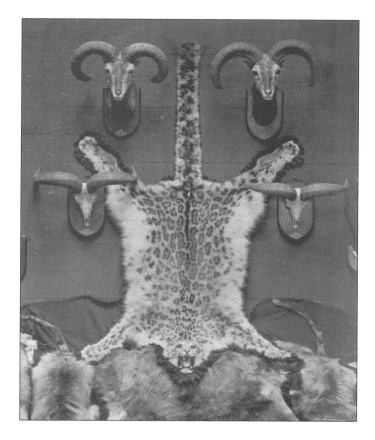

Rugs and wall- mounted skins often formed part of a large batch of hunting trophies. Gerrard's photo albums included many examples of this, mostly showing African species (below). Occasionally they prepared a batch of trophies from Asia, like those (top right) which included a snow leopard rug.

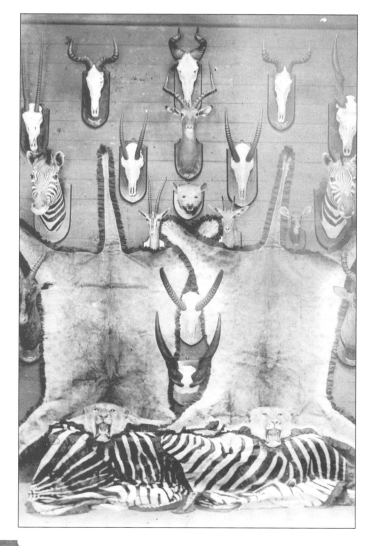

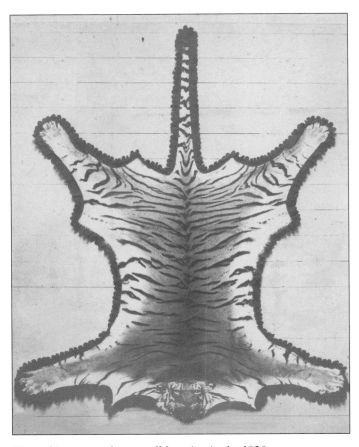

Tiger skin prepared as a wall hanging in the 1920s.

Rug Prices

Prices of rugs, dressed, trimmed with felt and lined with canvas. This price included modelling the head with the mouth open. In comparison, in 1932 a police constable earned about 85/- per week.

NB £1= 20/-

Species	1932	1951 (excl. tax)
Lion, tiger	180/- to 240/-	300/- +
Leopard, puma	100/- to 120/-	240/-
Bears	100/- to 200/-	
Hyena, dog, lynx	60/- to 80/-	
Fox, badger, otter	40/- to 55/-	

Muffs, slippers, wraps, stoles and gauntlets added to the range of furry items that Gerrards would make, often to special order. The firm even advertised its ability to supply leopard skins "as drummers aprons", although this must have been a very limited market. Even in 1951, wartime rationing was still in force for many items, including clothes. Customers needed the requisite number of clothing coupons to buy gloves and similar items, even if they were only made of rabbit fur. This market must also have been limited as a result.

In time, the rug business expanded to include not just rugs made from skins, but other materials too. However, ultimately it was the rug business that finally brought Gerrards to financial collapse.

Typical tiger skin rugs with felt edging and modelled heads. Such skins are still seen today in the antiques trade, although they are often very faded. Tiger skins may be sold legally in Britain if they date from before 1947.

Clothing and trinkets

Feathers were supplied made into hats and trimmings for coat collars and gloves. Gerrards price lists also offered feather fans, including some made from dyed ostrich. Shoes and slippers were also available, made to order from snake, ostrich and zebra skin. They cost upwards of 30/-. Antelope, snake, lizard, rhino, elephant ear, and crocodile skins could be made into belts, braces, purses (costing 7/6d in 1932), tobacco pouches (12/6d) and letter wallets (£1-15/-). Handbags (from £2-10/-), blotting books, cigar cases (15/6d), skin-covered boxes, visitors books and similar items were also offered. Rhino hide walking sticks were popular too. Bangles of elephant hair were available, with the same material being offered fashioned into wrist watch straps. Elephant toenails could be made into ash trays too, costing 12/- in 1932. It seems that nothing was too trivial and nothing was wasted from the skins and bodies that arrived at the yard.

It is hard to believe that such a variety of specialist products were all made on site. Perhaps at least some of them were contracted out, if and when any orders materialised. No doubt if a particular line proved popular, steps would have been taken to manufacture it in house.

A specially delicate line was the manufacture of brooches and tie pins made from 'lucky bones'. These are clavicles ('collar bones'), which are reduced to tiny vestigial structures in members of the cat family. Those from lions and tigers were highly prized by big game hunters and regarded as magical charms among the

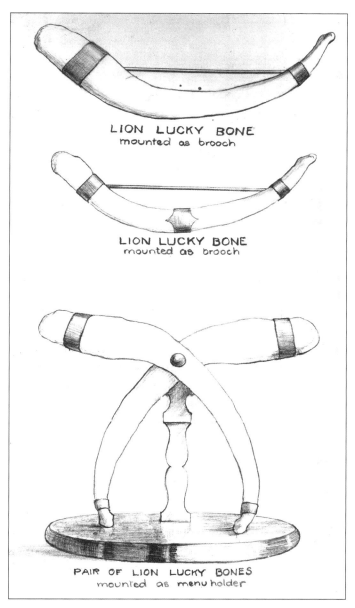

Artwork prepared for a catalogue, but probably not used, illustrating mounted lion lucky bones.

native people of India. They would be cut from the freshly skinned carcass, rough cleaned and then sent to a taxidermist or jewellers to be mounted on a metal pin as a souvenir of a successful hunt.

Gerrard's price lists show lucky bones among their many non-taxidermy products. In 1932 they cost £1/10/-, gold mounted as brooches, but were only priced at 7/6d in 1921. The difference could be due to price inflation with time, but is more likely because the earlier ones were not gold mounted but set in some less expensive material.

There is of course a basic illogicality about these and other lucky charms made from animals. After all, the animal had two of them and still finished up being shot.

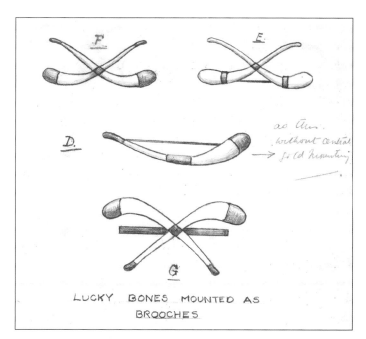

Annotated artwork showing lion lucky bones made into various types of brooches.

TIGER, LION, AND LEOPARD CLAWS.

Mounted as Menu Holders	…	…	…	from 10/-
,, ,, Brooches	..	…	…	,, 7/6
,, ,, Shawl Pins	…	…	…	,, 15/-
,, ,, Charms and Pins	…	…	…	,, 6/-
,, ,, Belt Clasps and Buckles of 2 or 4 Claws				,, 21/-
,, ,, Liqueur, Spirit, or Wine Labels		…		,, 10/6

Various designs submitted.

Lion, Tiger, and Panther Lucky Bones, Pins, and Brooches … … … … … ,, 7/6

Part of a 1921 price list showing tiger and leopard claws made into brooches etc.

Wallets, suitcases and document pouches could be supplied, tastefully covered with snake or lizard skin. The boxes and suitcases were probably not made from scratch, but based on ordinary commercially available products, with the skin being applied to the outside at Gerrards.

Birds

Chapter 8
Birds

Birds were prepared from freshly-dead specimens or from dried cabinet skins. The latter can usually be dampened down sufficiently to remodel them successfully. However, very old specimens, or those that have lain on their back for decades, often have the feathers flattened or distorted and this is difficult to conceal when the bird is remounted in a different position. If the original skin was fatty (as was often the case with water birds or with migrants killed in the autumn) the fat would often oxidise, resulting in the skin becoming fragile and crumbling away. Remounting such specimens is often impossible.

Customers were urged to send fresh dead birds by post, taking care to first plug the nostrils with small wads of cotton wool. This was to avoid spoiling the specimens as a result of blood or other fluids leaking out and contaminating the feathers. Staining the feathers would make it more difficult to do a good job on the bird later. It was the problem of variable condition that led Gerrards to qualify their price lists by insisting they were only meant as guidance and that the actual cost of taxidermy would depend on the work involved.

Birds of Paradise were normally obtained only as dried cabinet skins and they still looked stiff and wooden even after being softened up and mounted.

Prices for preparing birds from fresh specimens or dried skins

Species	1921 bird supplied by customer	1951 bird supplied by customer	1951 'off the shelf'
Finch	2/-	15/-	32/6d
Blackbird	3/-	22/6d	42/6d
Pigeon	4/6d		
Partridge	6/-		
Gulls	5/-		
Pheasant	10/-	38/6d	
Wren	12/6d	25/-	
King penguin	80/-		
Humming bird	12/6d		
Cabinet skin: thrush size	1/-	5/-	

A woodcock- the last bird by Gerrard's last taxidermist, Horace Owen. It has a body formed from tightly bound wood wool, the wings are supported by wires bound to the bones. Unusually, there are two wires in the neck, seen in X-ray below.

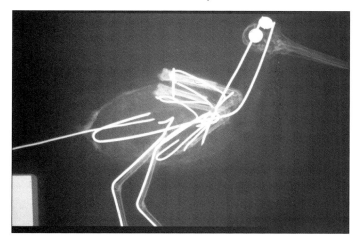

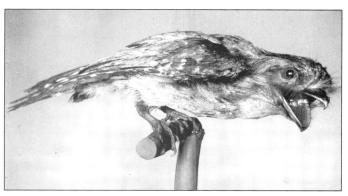

The least expensive bird mounts were where the specimen was set up on a simple twig (like the hawfinch, top) or T or inverted L shaped perch (like the tawny frogmouth, above), without a glass case or elaborate rockwork.

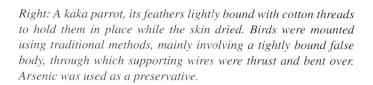

Right: A kaka parrot, its feathers lightly bound with cotton threads to hold them in place while the skin dried. Birds were mounted using traditional methods, mainly involving a tightly bound false body, through which supporting wires were thrust and bent over. Arsenic was used as a preservative.

Ted Paul 'The Bird Man' one of the taxidermists in the 1950s, seen here with a condor and holding a shrike.

Above: This extraordinary arrangement shows a brown kiwi, its skeleton and an egg, set up for display within an oval glass dome. Kiwis lay the largest eggs in proportion to their size, of any bird. Their skeleton is interesting too, but this still seems an odd way to display these features. Perhaps there was only one size of glass dome available in the store.

Small birds were trussed in cotton threads while they dried, like those on the shelf in the background here. 'Flying' birds had the plumage supported by strips of paper pinned to the mount. These would hold the feathers in position while the bird dried, after which the feathers would remain as they were arranged by the taxidermist (in this case a man named Wood).

Some of Gerrard's work was done for museums. Habitat groups of birds, like these showing curlews and black headed gulls, would be set up in the workshop then fully assembled in their display case on site. The gulls were evidently considered to be a particularly successful example as this photograph (taken in Gerrard's yard) featured in a small advertising leaflet issued during the inter-war years.

Some Gerrard case styles

Neat glass cases were available and in 1921, ranged from 7/6d for a finch-sized bird to 25/- or more for birds the size of a pheasant. For all species, there was a small additional charge for mounting a bird with outstretched wings. By way of comparison, in the 1960s, Rowland Ward Ltd charged about £5 just for mounting a small bird without a case.

In his unpublished book, a third of which was about bird taxidermy, Charles Gerrard claimed to have prepared "everything from ostriches to hummingbirds" and recommended skinning birds through an incision under the wing. His text made frequent reference to using "insect powder" as a skin preservative. This was in fact DDT powder, available in those days for killing insects about the house. Dried moss was described as "Very handy for covering errors, heads of nails, uncovered paper etc".

A peregrine and its prey in a glass-sided case.

Hobby in a typical glass fronted box, the commonest and least expensive display case used by Gerrards. Sometimes, as here, gilded fillet was added to the outside. X-rays reveal that this bird was mounted as a 'bind up' (based on a mass of tow, tightly bound with tough thread to form the false body). A thick central wire was pushed through, bent back and clinched into the body. A separate wire supports the tail. The wings were also wired separately, and mounting them outsretched like this meant an additional cost. The wing bones were cut at the elbows and legs were severed at the top of tibia. A lead pellet lodged in the skull suggests that the bird was originally shot, perhaps by a gamekeeper.

An all-glass case containing a male passenger pigeon mounted by Charles Gerrard from a cabinet skin (note the flattened feathers, where the bird had previously lain for years on its back)

Cases with glass side panels were more expensive, but created a lighter and more airy display, as for this buzzard example.

An early all-glass case with bent glass top. This elegant, but expensive style had the drawback that it was almost impossible to replace the top panel if it got broken.

An oval glass dome of Scots owls by Gerrards.

An umbrella bird (and other South American species) in a case with glass top and sides.

An attractive late 19th century case of extinct huias from New Zealand. This case was sold at Sothebys (on behalf of Gerrards) for £520 in 1971 and spent 30 years in Scotland. It was then bought by the Victorian Taxidermy Company and sold for over £15,000.

Above and left: Late 19th century octagonal cases, similar to some that were produced by Henry Ward of London.

An unusual Gerrard case, having the side panels and back of the case painted to look like surrounding reeds. The swan is supported on a pane of glass that represents the water surface.

Fish and other Vertebrates

Chapter 9
Fish and other Vertebrates

Fish were another of Gerrard's products, although they are not as common today, as those of the specialist contemporary London fish taxidermists (such as Cooper, Homer and Anstiss). Some fish were prepared as plaster casts (particularly species with a gelatinous body that was hard to skin). These cost about the same as stuffed fish, up to a length of about 1m (40 inches). Thereafter they became substantially more expensive, probably due to the increased amounts of material needed and the practical problems of handling and casting large objects (see Table opposite). Carved wooden models were offered to customers at one time, but cost nearly three times as much as skin mounts, and I have never seen an example by Gerrards.

Gerrards guaranteed that their mounted fish would be the correct size, as a plaster impression was taken as soon as the fish reached the workshop. This served as a mould into which the skin could be fitted and then packed with sawdust around a central wooden block. Once the skin was dry, the fish was removed from its plaster jacket and suitably coloured. Silvery fish had silver paint or foil added first, with coloured varnishes on top.

Later sales brochures advertised that Gerrard's skin mounts and casts were accurately coloured once they were dry. However, where colouring was not deemed necessary, the skin was left unpainted and dried to a pale brown. Gerrards did not use oil paints, just artist's powder colours made up with industrial methylated spirits and white or brown button polish (shellac- a type of varnish). This mixture soaks well into plaster and skin, but is prone to flaking off shiny surfaces such as scales.

Charles Gerrard working on fish, applying colour to a skin mount.   © *Mirrorpix*

Charles Gerrard applying a silver finish to the fish before adding a layer of colour over the top.

Three typical styles of fish mount by Gerrards

A skin mount attached to a back board. This fish was stuffed with sawdust around a central wooden support.

In his unpublished book, Charles Gerrard commented "Water colours are not suitable being too thin even the driest and most non-greasy taxidermy specimens do not take kindly to water colours. Oil colours are excellent and should be used whenever possible. Powder paints are the most convenient if kept in a box with a well fitting lid and divided into compartments for the different colours. There will be little likelihood of the colours spilling. Powder colours may be mixed with methylated spirit on to a palette and for hardening, white polish should be used for the lighter colours and button or brown polish for the darker ones. Soft haired brushes are not suitable for powder painting and stiffer hair is called for and a supply of various sizes will be useful … Avoid black whenever possible as it is extremely light and liable to blow away". He also advised that a taxidermist who intended to eat the flesh of a fish that was being skinned, should take care to avoid its contamination with poisonous chemicals. He suggested "Try a little on the cat, he will know!"

This is a plaster cast mounted on a wooden back board. Cast were particularly suitable for fish with a thin, scale-less skin and very smooth body.

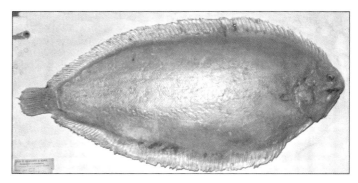

This sole is a skin mount, but filled with plaster to make a smooth, solid, but very heavy specimen.

Gerrard's fish prices in 1951			
Size (inches)	Mounted	Plaster cast	Wooden model
12	£ 1/15/-	£ 1/15/-	
36	£ 4/15/-	£ 4/15/-	£ 9/10/-
48	£ 6/10/-	£ 7/15/-	£13/10/-
60	£10/ 00/-	£15/10/-	£22/00/-

As an amusing illustration of the quality of their work, one Gerrard brochure told proudly how some of their fish were taken to the Wembley Exhibition. Here, some salmon mounts were spoiled by exhibition staff picking them up to weigh alongside fresh fish. The people were said not to have realised that the fish were taxidermy specimens, and not the real thing, until the paint came off!

In 1921, Gerrard's fish prices ranged from 12/- for a 1lb fish to 45/- for a 10lb fish, up to £5 for one weighing 30lb. These prices included a plain case with flat glass front. Bow fronted cases cost about 30% extra. The specialist London fish taxidermist W.F. Homer issued a price list in about 1930 which showed the cost of the same three sizes of fish, in flat fronted cases, as 22/-, 75/- and £8/14/-. Gerrards were evidently at least one third cheaper, allowing for price inflation between 1921 and the 1930s. According to his price lists, Homer also charged about 20-25% more for a bow-fronted case than a flat fronted one.

Fish sizes were defined by weight rather than length, probably because that was how anglers rated them. However, to a taxidermist, the length is probably more important for various practical reasons (including the cost of glass and wood, a long fish requiring a larger case than a heavier fish that was shorter in body length). By 1951, Gerrard's prices had been redefined accordingly and were related to body length (see Table).

Also in 1951, Gerrards offered tunny fish tails (upright) on wooden plaques at a cost of £6/10/-. A tunny head mounted on shield was £20, and without the shield £17. Salmon and pike heads cost upwards of £3 each, but £1 less without a shield. Sign writing in gold lettering, shaded in black, was offered for whole fish and fish head mounts at 3d per letter, or shaded in white for 2d per letter.

Pictures from Gerrard's photo album showing some examples of their fish. They range from a display in a major public museum to the barracuda and tarpon heads mounted on typical Gerrard shields, similar to those used for mammal head mounts.

Other Vertebrates

There has never been much demand for stuffed reptiles or amphibians, and the latter are rarely a success anyway. Nevertheless, some reptiles and a few frogs and toads were prepared by Gerrards, using normal taxidermy techniques, modified as necessary. Since frogs have no fur or feathers under which to hide a line of stitches, they would have been skinned by turning them inside out through the mouth rather than through a mid ventral incision. They were then filled with sawdust or cotton wool, but this tended to make them look very plump, even species that appear lean and slender in life. They also needed to be coloured, but paint applied to the skin is a poor substitute for the dermal pigmentation found in living amphibia. For these reasons, stuffed amphibians were rarely produced and models made by casting the animals in plaster provided a more attractive alternative.

Reptiles have a tough skin and rarely need subtle colouring to look reasonably realistic. Since they characteristically sprawl on their belly, they could also be skinned through a normal incision and mounted with the stitching hidden underneath (although snakes were usually skinned through the mouth). Like other taxidermists, Gerrards seem to have done relatively few reptiles, but they did make use of dead animals from zoos to create specimens for museum displays and Charles Gerrard was a friend of C.P. Ionides (the 'African snake man'), who sent him live snakes though the post. Gerrards also offered a range of clothing and accessories made from reptiles (especially python skins), ranging from shoes to handbags.

Skin mount of a chimaera ('rat fish'), on a board.

Even though there were better and more famous fish taxidermists in London, Gerrards still managed to attract business from relatively wealthy customers like the man here (fishing for tarpon doesn't come cheap), but who was he?

An ocean sunfish, a species that does not make good skin mounts. If the skin wrinkles as it dries it creates a very unnatural rough surface and edges to what is a naturally sleek fish.

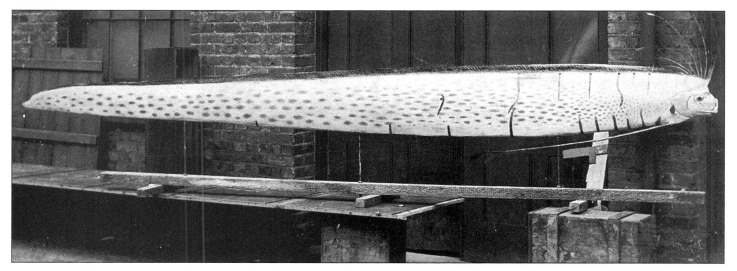

A specimen of the mysterious oarfish, prepared by Gerrards and photographed in their yard.

Other Vertebrates

A large python by Gerrards. The python is posed on an artificial tree trunk, probably made from wire and paper. Mounted snakes often suffered from their scales warping and lifting as they dried, spoiling their characteristic smooth and streamlined appearance, but that appears not to have happened with this specimen.

Giant tortoises by Gerrards.

Prepared tortoises are quite common. There isn't much that can go wrong with them and they rarely need additional colouring.

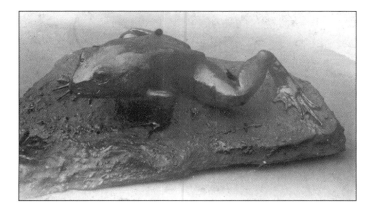

Stuffed frogs tend to look bloated, especially those species that are lean, angular and athletic-looking in life. This makes them unsuitable as display items.

Charles Gerrard inspecting a dead grass snake. As usual, there is plenty of clutter about, in this case including a bind-up manikin for a fox mask.

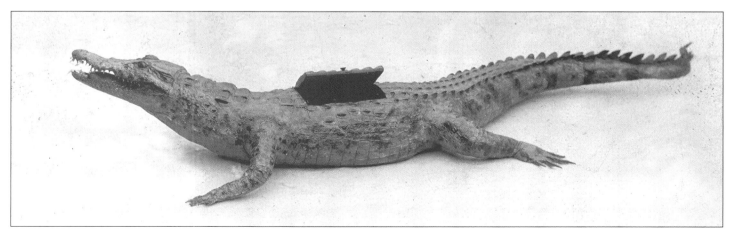

This small crocodile seems to have been modified to form a matchbox or small trinket case

A Record Tunny by Gerrards

This tunny fish, weighing 763lb (346kg) was caught by Colonel George Baker in 1933 some 25 miles off the Yorkshire coast at Scarborough. It took him almost five hours to land using a Hardy Saltwater no.5 cane rod and 54 thread line, a feat which gained him the Paul Latham Trophy and Hardy Cup for best fish of the year caught on rod and line. The head was mounted and coloured by Gerrards for £15, including the oak shield and inscription. The tail was mounted separately on a smaller shield for £2. Packing and delivery cost £1-15/-, with £1 offered for return of the box. The head was sold at auction for £3,400 in October 1994 and exhibited at Mr Potter's Museum of Curiosities in Cornwall until 2003, when it was sold again to The Victorian Taxidermy Company for just over £4,800.

Despite the interest in tunny fishing off the British coast in the 1930s, few were actually caught. Two were preserved by Gerrards, this one and the head of another, now in the Scarborough Museum, caught in 1949 by J.H.Lewis of Lincoln.

This is a skin mount trophy head, with the original bill dated 1933, which includes an offer to refund £1 if the box was returned. Old boxes were worth having as they could be used again for future deliveries or sawn up in the workshop to become part of the supporting framework inside large mammal and fish mounts.

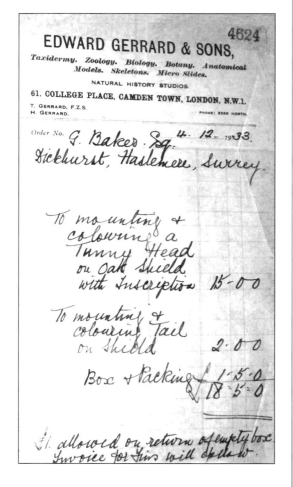

Osteology and Model Making

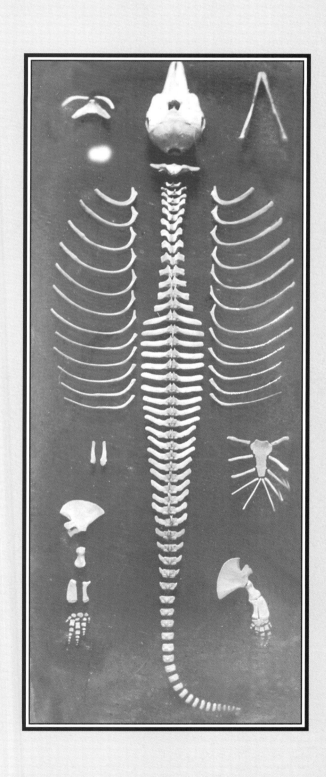

Chapter 10
Osteology and Model Making

Preparing and articulating skeletons was a speciality of the first Edward Gerrard, a tradition that continued in the family business. Skulls and skeletons were much in demand for teaching human and comparative anatomy, often with special modifications such as the removal of bone to show developing teeth or the addition of model muscles and blood vessels. Edward Gerrard & Sons remained the principal suppliers of such material until the mid 20th century, by which time this line of work had been almost entirely taken over by their sister company T. Gerrard & Co.

A special line, combining Gerrard's expertise in osteological preparation with their skills in modelling, consisted of articulated skeletons with the left or right half covered by the skin (or a shell of false skin made from papier maché) and lined with black velvet. Some of these may have been imported from Germany, but others were made by Gerrards, possibly including the walking man and horse at the Natural History Museum in London, and others in The Horniman Museum and in Dublin.

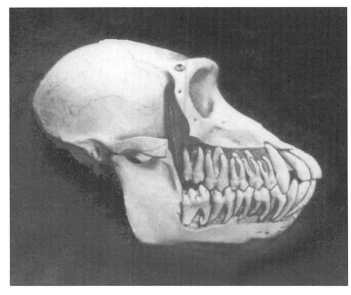

The skull of an ape with part of the maxilla and mandible removed to show the teeth in situ

Setting up a skeleton, like this kiwi, was a time consuming and skilled job, similar to assembling a three-dimensional jigsaw puzzle. First the bones had to be cleaned of flesh and then bleached, but the more thoroughly this was done, the more the bones separated and the longer it took to put them together again. A detailed knowledge of anatomy was essential in order to distinguish right and left components of the skeleton and to attain a lifelike posture. The best skeletons had bones joined by wires, cheaper ones had them glued together. Bird skeletons were easier to prepare than mammals, as the latter have more bones (about 200 in a human). Snakes and fish were difficult too, since they have large numbers of bones that all look the same.

Charles Gerrard fitting together the bones of a left foot.

One of the female staff threading a python skull on to the central wire of a skeleton to complete the specimen. This photograph was taken in 1934, before the separation of T. Gerrard's osteological business from the parent company. (©*Hulton-Deutsch/CORBIS*)

Here a staff member at Gerrards (still wearing his trilby hat!) is scraping the flesh off a snake skeleton, with various other roughly cleaned specimens lying on the bench. The photograph was taken in 1950, so this type of work was still being done long after T. Gerrard & Co. Ltd had set up separately, specialising in osteological preparations. Snake skeletons have large numbers of bones that are difficult to sort out if they become separated. The vertebrae and roughly cleaned ribs were therefore threaded on to a length of wire before fully cleaning and bleaching the skeleton. (©*Hulton-Deutsch/CORBIS*)

Below: the disarticulated skeleton of a porpoise, laid out for decorative effect. Cetaceans have only a rudimentary pelvis (visible in this picture as two small bars just to the right of centre). The tail tapers off to a blunt end.

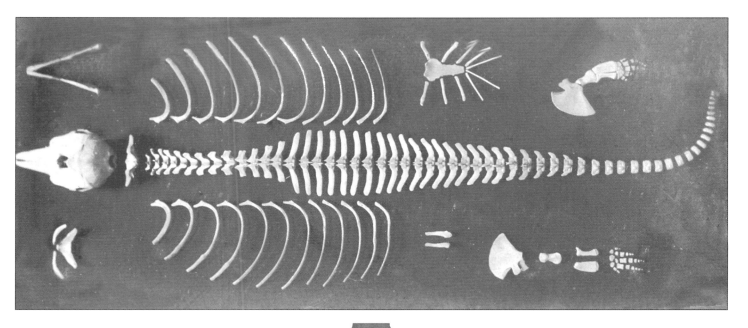

Gerrards used plaster of Paris to build a model of the skeleton of an extinct giant armadillo, the size of a small car. One side of the carapace was removed to reveal the structure inside. The same style was followed when Gerrards built a model of the extinct giant ground sloth (*Megatherium*), some 3.5m tall. This stood on its hind legs against a tree in the Dome of Discovery at the Festival of Britain in 1951. It is one of the most impressive things I remember from a schoolboy visit there with my parents. It was clad in shaggy brown fur on one side, but had the skeleton exposed on the other. It was probably the largest model ever made by Gerrards.

A newspaper interview for the News Chronicle, about 1950, reported that Gerrards were making not only the giant Megatherium model, but also an artificial leg for someone's pet alligator. The animal had apparently bitten off one of its real ones.

Model making seems not only to have been in demand by museums, but also commercially for special exhibitions. Models were also used in various types of teaching (instructing people in matters to do with hygiene and disease transmission for example), and some can still be seen in the Wellcome Museum of Tropical Medicine in London. Gerrard's models ranged from huge fleas and house flies to a full sized cow prepared for an exhibition as part of a display about dairy produce. This embodied the special and unique qualities of Gerrards, the taxidermy being done by Charles, with Ted's skill employed to make the cow's head move and for the udder to deliver quantities of 'milk'.

However, ingenuity also had its drawbacks and Charles Gerrard was fond of telling a story concerning a major soap manufacturer who wanted a model oil palm tree for an exhibition. Charles made one, creating bunches of 'ripe fruits' from bundles of crocus bulbs sealed with shellac. Everyone was very pleased, until an alarmed telephone call came through a few days after the exhibition had opened to say that in the warm and humid conditions of the exhibition hall the bulbs had begun to sprout!

Models of British reptiles and amphibians, in the form of plaster casts, were a more modest offering, produced in significant numbers. They ranged in price (in 1951) from 17/6d for a newt or natterjack toad, up to £3 for an adder, smooth snake or grass snake. Once a suitable mould had been made, making multiple casts from it cost relatively little in time or materials (the main cost was in painting the model). By 1951, the range of models was being extended and already included interesting foreign species such as the tuatara (*Sphenodon*) and

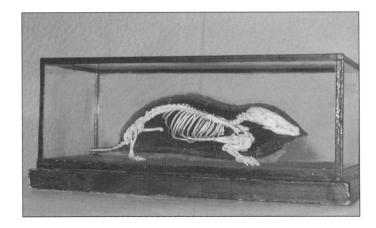

A typical Gerrard product, combining taxidermy with osteology. This mole skeleton has the skin wrapped round half of it, so that from one side the animal appears complete, as in life, but seen from the other side, the skeleton's relationship with the outside appearance is revealed. Seen from above, the 'half and half' nature of the object is very clear.

Gila monster (*Heloderma*), no doubt using fresh dead specimens from a zoo. The advantage of these models lay in the fact that conventional taxidermy techniques tend to give disappointing results, especially with amphibians, in which both the natural colouring and shape are lost. Another alternative, specimens preserved in formalin, are also unsatisfactory as they often become distorted and always lose their natural colours.

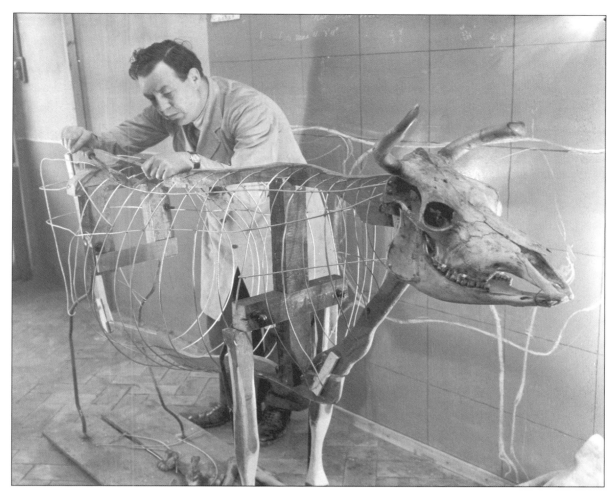

Charles Gerrard working on a model cow. An outline was drawn on the adjacent wall to ensure the correct size and proportions were maintained.

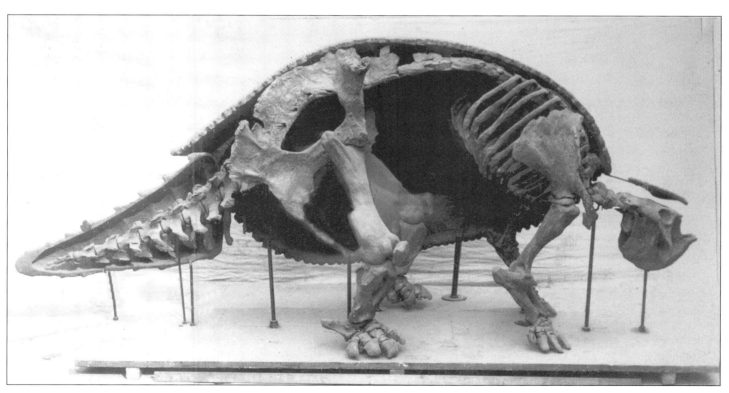

Life sized model of a giant armadillo, made from plaster. The skeleton is displayed within half the carapace. Similar models were offered to museums by Ward's Natural Science Establishment in America.

The tale of a whale's tail

Charles Gerrard was one of the team that prepared the bones of a 90ft (27m) blue whale for the Natural History Museum in London. The others were Ted Gerrard, Charlie Bush and G. Pethard. (Charlie Bush later became Chief Articulator at the Royal College of Surgeons of England, where some of his work can still be seen in the Hunterian Museum).

The fully articulated whale skeleton was to be suspended from the ceiling, high above a full sized model of the animal in life. This was made in 1937 by a team of plasterers supervised by Stuart Stammwitz (not Gerrards), based on a wood and wire mesh body (Snell & Tucker, 2003). Charles was fond of telling how he found the coccyx (fused terminal vertebrae) from the whale in his brown overall pocket long after the skeleton had been winched up into place and the scaffolding giving access had been removed. He gave it to a friend and the skeleton remains incomplete to this day.

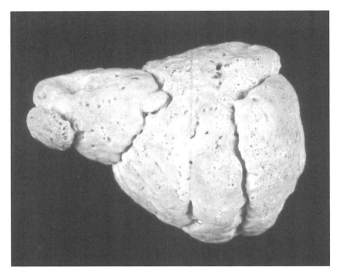

The whale's coccyx (fused terminal tail vertebrae) that Charles Gerrard found in his pocket after the task of articulating and positioning the skeleton was completed. It is about 4cm long.

Above: painted plaster models of various species of amphibians, including a salamander, two toads and two frogs.

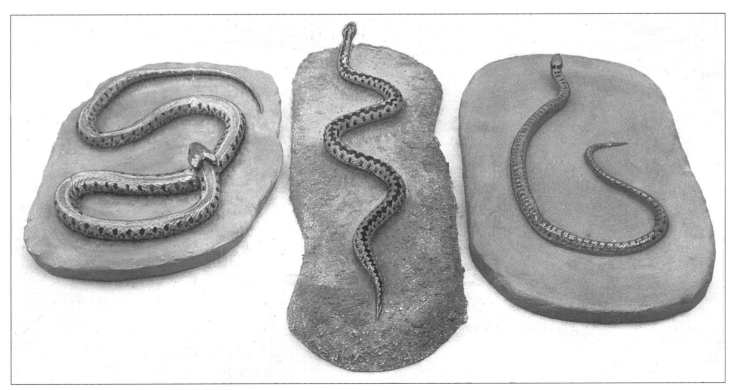

Painted plaster casts of all three British snakes- grass snake, adder and smooth snake.

Some advertisements and models dating from the 1930s.

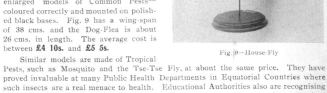

EDWARD GERRARD & SONS

HEALTH & HYGIENE MODELS (PESTS)

These we make to order and are not usually supplied from stock. The simplest kind are in figures 9 and 10. These are enlarged models of Common Pests—coloured correctly and mounted on polished black bases. Fig. 9 has a wing-span of 38 cms. and the Dog-Flea is about 26 cms. in length. The average cost is between **£4 10s.** and **£5 5s.**

Similar models are made of Tropical Pests, such as Mosquito and the Tse-Tse Fly, at about the same price. They have proved invaluable at many Public Health Departments in Equatorial Countries where such insects are a real menace to health. Educational Authorities also are recognising the value of enlarged models of dangerous Pests, and most Museums have acquired models relevant to the problems of the surrounding country.

Please write for further details.

Fig. 9—House-Fly

FOOD MODELS

In connection with the House-Fly Model, we often supply realistic imitations of cooked and uncooked foods to illustrate the occurrence and prevention of contamination. This series is not complete without a small model showing the Fly scavenging over a dust-heap.

DISEASE MODELS

These are wax mouldings on wooden boards, and they can be supplied to show the characteristic appearances of industrial, sexual, and infantile diseases.

(Price List M. 187/38/4)

Fig. 10—Adult Dog-Flea

LONDON, ENGLAND   Telephone: EUSton 2765

Charles Gerrard using a microscope to examine details of a flea while building an enlarged model of one, as shown in the advertisement (top left). (Hulton Archive/ Getty Images).

A relief model showing the characteristics of different types of parasitic worms found in various parts of a chicken. For a long time, such topics were part of the sixth form biology curriculum, as well as being of interest to vets, trainee farmers and animal managers.

EDWARD GERRARD & SONS

ANATOMICAL MODELS (HUMAN)

We need not remind you of of the advantages of teaching this important subject with the aid of a few simple, scientifically—correct models.

These can be made to illustrate the complicated structures and mechanisms of the human body in a way that is helpful to the Lecturer and to the Student, and incidentally save time.

There are three types of Human Models:—
(1) Solid Non-Dissectible.
(2) Solid, but with hinged sections.
(3) Fully Dissectible.

The first style is shown in Fig.6—Section of Human Head on board. Each part of this is coloured and numbered. The price with key is **£2 10s.**

Fig. 6—Section Head

TRUNK MODELS

Full-size models of the Human Trunk can be supplied in many different styles, with or without heads, dissectible or non-dissectible. The more popular models are mounted on boards with supports for setting upright.

The second style is illustrated by Fig. 7, which shows a useful model of the Human Heart, with apertures for inspecting auricle and ventricle. The price of this model is **£5**

They enable the Student to realize the inter-dependence of the organs and their relative positions. Further details will be sent on application.

Fig. 7—Heart (Human)

Fig. 8 shows the third style, this model being fully dissectible. The cochlea, ossicles and drum may be removed and examined separately. This is a very instructive model, cost **£3 5s.**

Many other models are available, showing details of :—

The Skin	Stomach
The Nose and Mouth	Intestines
The Eye	Digestive System
The Teeth	Nervous System
Larynx	etc., etc.
Lungs	*(Price List A.M. 186/38/4)*

Fig. 8—Ear (Human)

61, COLLEGE PLACE, N.W.1   Telephone: EUSton 2765

Also on offer were plaster models of dissected invertebrate (many times bigger than natural size) and dissected organs such as sets of comparative brains.

Models of disease vectors, such as tsetse flies and mosquitoes, were used for teaching people, in Britain and abroad, which species were dangerous and how to recognise them. A model, vastly bigger than the real thing, is easier to see and to use for instructional purposes, especially with large groups of people and in the absence of microscopes. Models retained their structural integrity, whereas real insects are often distorted by the processes of preservation and mounting. Models were also available throughout the year and in any weather (unlike the real thing). These giant insects were made from wire, wax, Cellophane and bristles from various household brushes

Another class of models included representations of the life histories of various insects and also demonstrations of insect crop pests and the nature of the damage they cause. These were usually set up in display cases like those shown here, and included appropriate modelled vegetation and fruits.

Actual specimens, preserved in formalin and mounted in museum jars, were an alternative way of supplying teaching material, linked to topics covered in school and university syllabuses. Such specimens included dissected fish, and typical parasitic infestations. But this line of business was increasingly taken over by T.Gerrard & Co. with considerable success. By 1951, Edward Gerrard & Sons were no longer supplying live amphibians or specimens of them preserved in formalin

for dissection in schools. These too were supplied by T. Gerrard and Co, at high cost to populations of Britain's wild reptiles and amphibians. It was also at the cost of removing a lucrative line of business from Edward Gerrard & Sons.

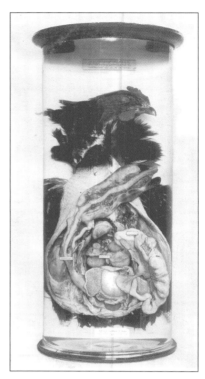

By 1951, Edward Gerrard & Sons had ceased to sell pickled display specimens of dissected animals in museum jars showing parasites and disease, like this preparation of a domestic fowl

Models of the life cycle of British butterflies, including the caterpillar and characteristic larval food plants, together with an actual specimen of the adult insect.

A model farm, built for display at an agricultural exhibition. Models like this could be used to demonstrate particular methods of housing and managing livestock

An Assessment

Chapter 11
An Assessment

Gerrards was established in the heyday of British taxidermy and faced many direct competitors in London alone. These included the large business of James Gardner (with a Royal Warrant and premises in Oxford Street) and several other high profile taxidermists, with important social connections and businesses that lasted for decades. They also included the specialist fish taxidermist John Cooper and Sons, whose work was regarded as the finest available, and various bird specialists such as the London taxidermists Leadbeater, Dawes and Burton, all of whom were capable of producing high quality work, easily as good as Gerrard's.

However, none of these other taxidermists did large mammals, few attempted game trophy heads and fewer still offered osteological preparations and biological models (in demand by museums and educational institutions). Most of these smaller businesses had closed by the time of the First World War, regardless of the superior quality of taxidermy that some of them had produced.

From about 1880, Rowland Ward Ltd was unquestionably the leading London taxidermist and Edward Gerrard & Sons operated in direct competition with them, particularly in the area of big game trophies,

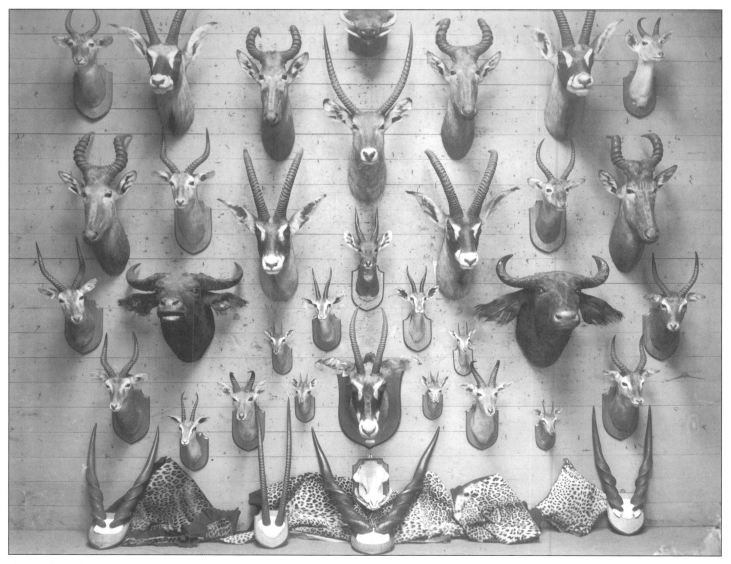

Gerrards produced vast numbers of game trophy heads, but few other taxidermists did them at all.

whole mammal mounts and animal furniture. Indeed the items offered by the two companies were almost identical. Gerrards was established earlier (in 1850), but the business of Rowland Ward had grown out of that set up by his father Henry, who in turn had begun about the same time as the first Edward Gerrard.

Rowland Ward had a reputation for higher quality than Gerrards, but also higher prices. Although I have not been able to trace exactly comparable price lists, the cost of mounting a small bird such as a sparrow in the 1960s was four to six times as much if it was done by Wards rather than Gerrards (who charged only 15/- in the 1950s). A similar fourfold price differential is evident when comparing the cost of providing a glass case for it. A Gerrard glass case would have cost about 10/- in the 1950s, Ward's charged £3 in the 1960s. But Ward's cases were all-glass and likely to have been more expensive to make than the simple glass fronted boxes often supplied by Gerrards. Nevertheless, however much buyers might like superior styles and appearance, money is money and the lower cost of Gerrard products could have been a decisive factor for many of their customers.

Both companies enjoyed the services of very loyal and experienced staff, several of whom worked in the business to well beyond normal retiring age. Both companies also had loyal customers who were evidently pleased with what they got for their money. Both companies invested in advertising, but Wards did so widely and frequently in the national Press, whereas Gerrards rarely advertised at all, except in relatively obscure places such as the London Zoo guidebook. Unlike Wards, they also did not benefit from the publicity and status associated with publishing highly respected books by famous explorers and sportsmen, nor did they offer anything comparable with Ward's '*Sportsman's*

Handbook', giving instructions on how to prepare trophies in the field (and who to send them to of course!).

It is also clear that Rowland Ward was a master at manipulating the Press to his own advantage (Morris, 2003), whereas Gerrards appear to have done little more than grant occasional newspaper interviews on request. Wards had a prominent shop in Piccadilly and several of the other London taxidermists also had shops in the fashionable West End. By contrast, Gerrards had no shop at all and instead operated out of an obscure yard in Camden Town, never an easy part of London to reach. All of this must surely have contributed to Gerrard's substantially lower profile in the taxidermy business.

In terms of taxidermy, Rowland Ward Ltd often created very large mounts and museum groups. Gerrards did less of this type of work, lacking the necessary space (although they did mount the occasional elephants and rhinos).

Gerrards produced a full range of animal products. Hippos and rhinos offered endless scope for ingenuity, from whole mounts to furniture and ornaments

A pantomime horse in Gerrard's yard, doing nothing to enhance their reputation for good taxidermy. But few other taxidermists would have been bold enough to undertake such a job at all.

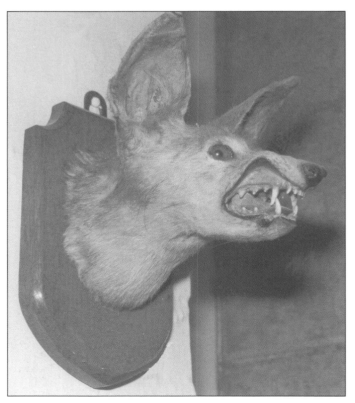

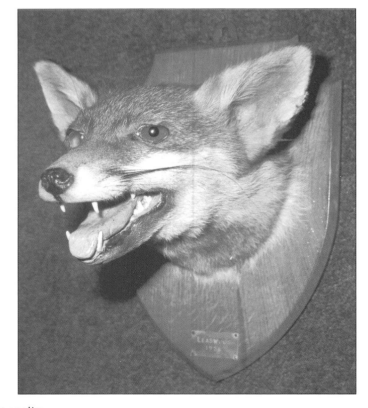

Some comparative examples of Gerrard products, showing inconsistent quality.

It has to be said that, compared to the products of Rowland Ward Ltd, the market leaders, some of the output from Gerrards was of inferior quality. This may have been due to a less rigorously imposed system of quality control, or it may have resulted from having a smaller workforce. With at least three times as many employees, Ward's were able to operate a production line system with specialist staff being dedicated to particular tasks such as 'finishing' (painting lips and eyelids and the fine modelling of facial details for example), so that individual workers became highly skilled at putting the finishing touches to specimens. Moreover, Ward's went to considerable lengths to achieve the highest possible standards (through the use of plaster death masks for example, rather than just relying on photographs to guide the finishers).

However, it would be unfair and incorrect to characterise Gerrard taxidermy as second rate because some of their products were very fine indeed. The difference between these two leading companies seems to have been more a question of consistency. While both Wards and Gerrards often produced items that we would even now consider as highly competent taxidermy, the former maintained a consistently high standard and the latter did not. It is rare even today to find a Ward product that looks badly done, but some Gerrard specimens appear to be very bad taxidermy indeed, especially to modern eyes. (the accompanying illustrations highlight the issue of inconsistency).

One area in which Gerrards excelled was in rug making and their tiger skin rugs are still seen in antiques sales today. Gerrards even did jobs on behalf of Rowland Ward Ltd, including the supply of crimped felt edging in various colours for Ward's own skin rugs.

Moreover, Gerrards were famously skilled model makers, but Ward's did not make models at all or do much osteological preparation (articulation of skeletons for example). Gerrards included these services, in spite of their smaller workforce. However, this must have further diluted the available talent, with each taxidermist having to cope with a very wide range of jobs and sometimes needing to help the model makers as well.

Some of Gerrard's bird cases, were very successful, showing both elegance and accurate taxidermy. Some of their other products showed neither.

The 1924 Empire Exhibition at Wembley

In 1924, the firm had a prominent stand at the British Empire Exhibition at Wembley, for which they were specially commended by the judges. Gerrard's display was set out either side of the map at the far end of the Kenya Court (see below and opposite). The Kenya Court was visited on May 28th by His Majesty King George Vth accompanied by Queen Mary. When they departed they signed a special visitors' book.

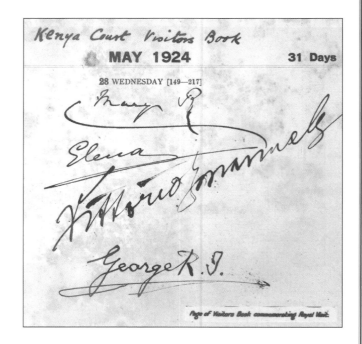

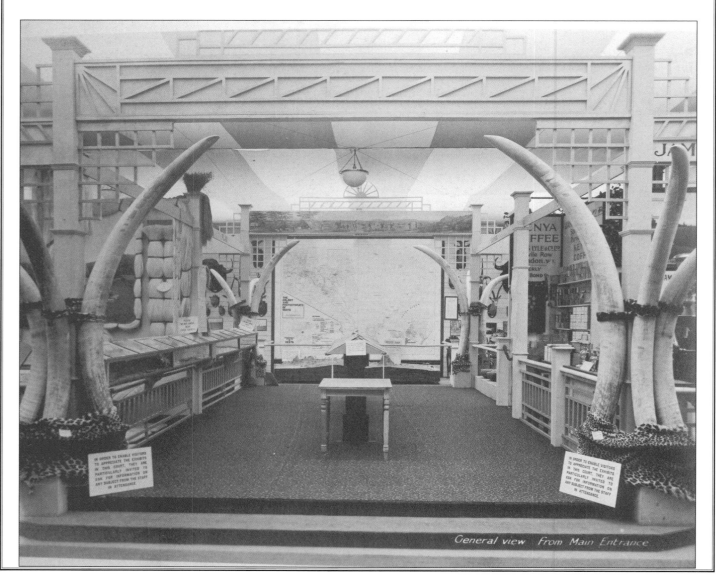

General view from Main Entrance

Gerrard's stand was set out on either side of a wall map at the Wembley Exhibition. His Majesty King George Vth spent a long time inspecting the display of trophy heads, rugs and photographs before leaving.

Success in versatility

The list of offerings in Gerrard's promotional literature was impressive, ranging from all sorts of taxidermy to furniture, shoes, gloves, rugs, silver plated ornaments and plaster casts. Indeed the list was so diverse, and sometimes so specialised, that it is hard to believe Gerrards could manufacture so many different things in the cramped and relatively small area of a single house and its back yard in Camden Town. They probably subcontracted various lines, should any customers actually order them, but some of their specialised services, particularly rug making, proved very popular. Moreover, Gerrards had almost a monopoly in the supply of casts, models and articulated skeletons, at least until these lines were taken over by T. Gerrard & Co after the Second World War.

All told, there was certainly enough to keep the business buoyant for decades, including the inter-War years and into the 1960s, despite the decline in popularity of taxidermy products. This diversity of work was the greatest strength of Gerrards and their most distinctive feature. No other British taxidermists, even Rowland Ward Ltd, ever matched the sheer variety of output achieved in the tiny cluttered yard behind 61 College Place.

Despite the many disadvantages that they faced, by the mid 20th century Edward Gerrard & Sons was clearly established as London's No. 2 taxidermists, second only to Rowland Ward Ltd. The quality of Gerrard's work was formally recognised by official commendations at many major exhibitions, in Britain and abroad. Various trade labels, company letterheads and brochures reminded customers that medals were awarded to the firm at exhibitions in Dublin, Moscow, Calcutta, and Adelaide, with more at the Indian & Colonial and Fisheries Exhibitions held in London. A gold medal was gained at the Paris Exhibition of 1900. Other exhibitions at which awards were made included St Louis (1904 and 1940), Franco-British (1908), Brussels (1910), Imperial (1911), Ghent (1913), Panama - Pacific (USA, 1915) and the Poultry Congress in Canada (1931). In 1924, the firm also had a prominent and highly commended display at the British Empire Exhibition at Wembley.

Apart from Rowland Ward, no other British taxidermists ever rivalled this record for both national and international recognition of their work.

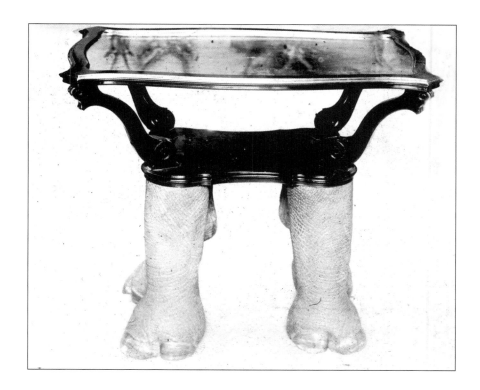

T. Gerrard & Co. Ltd.

Chapter 12
T. Gerrard & Co. Ltd.

Headed notepaper from 1933 shows the proprietors of Edward Gerrard & Sons to be Henry and Thomas Gerrard, evidently operating as equal partners, but with the latter specialising in osteological work and the former responsible for the taxidermy and hunting trophies. In 1938 Thomas Gerrard and his son Thomas Gerrard jnr. established a separate business, T. Gerrard & Co. Ltd, at 48 Pentonville Rd. London.

It is not clear why a separate business was set up. It was never listed separately in trade directories as a taxidermist, although specimens can sometimes be found bearing a T. Gerrard label. Perhaps he performed taxidermy in response to requests from his customers, or maybe he accepted commissions, but then farmed out the job to the Camden Town workshop.

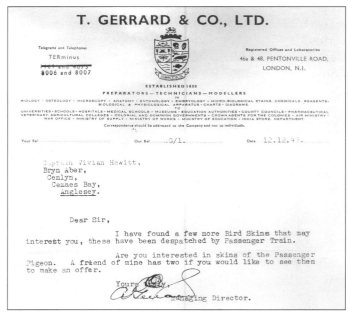

A letter to the avid collector Captain Vivian Hewitt, from which it is clear that T. Gerrard also dealt in bird skins.

This catalogue was the first issued by T. Gerrard after becoming a separate business in 1938. Inside it is dated 1935, with the name and address of Edward Gerrard & Sons on the title page, but with the new company's name and address applied as a supplementary label on the cover.

Thomas Gerrard was a Fellow of the Zoological Society of London, which doubtless provided him with many useful contacts and sources of specimens. He died in the late 1940s and was succeeded by his son, also called Thomas. Arthur Pethard, one of the men who worked on the whale skeleton for the Natural History Museum, transferred to T. Gerrard and later ran the business. This swiftly grew to become the principal British supplier of biological educational material. Huge numbers of dissections were prepared for schools, universities, medical schools and museums. The schools market expanded to include annual requests for dogfish, frogs and rats or rabbits, as these were core items in the sixth form curriculum until well into the 1960s, with a fresh generation of sixth formers needing specimens every year. At the same time, microscope slides were also required in large numbers as these too were vital teaching materials. As microscopy developed, so the firm needed to keep abreast of new techniques by employing more staff and specialist histochemists. Dissectors and osteological preparators needed to be trained too, as there was no obvious source from which to recruit them. At its peak the firm employed 40 specialist technicians.

Thomas Gerrard made an extensive overseas tour to drum up business and soon found many institutions willing to order material, including living cultures of

Protozoa, if the supply could be guaranteed and delivered on time. The business received a setback in 1940 when a bomb severely damaged the adjacent premises in Pentonville Road. But the War also brought contracts from the British and American Governments to supply medical preparations and specialised microscopical stains for the investigation and diagnosis of malaria. Servicemen apparently also brought home various interesting specimens that could be added to T. Gerrard's stock. At one stage during the War the London Zoo was ordered to divest itself of dangerous reptiles in case they escaped as a result of bomb damage in Regents Park. This doubtless provided useful material for Gerrard's other main line, namely skulls and articulated skeletons. This speciality had of course been a major strength within the parent company, but was then largely transferred to Thomas Gerrard.

In the post war years, standard osteological preparations continued to be made available, ranging from a guinea pig skeleton at £3 to a gorilla's for £100. The advance of technology also meant that preserved specimens were now available in Perspex boxes, rather than just glass, and the technique of freeze drying was also being introduced. Experiments were undertaken to replace Canada balsam, the traditional mountant used on microscope slides with the superior new material, methyl methacrylate. New resins were used to embed whole

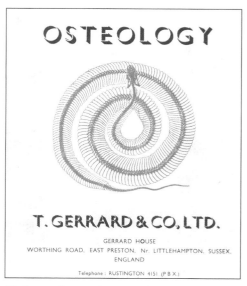

T. Gerrard's osteology catalogue of 1965

specimens, with a vacuum applied to remove air bubbles. Other new plastic materials were pressed into service to make valuable teaching aids in the form of larger than life size models of animals that could otherwise only be seen under the microscope. All this innovation required skilled technicians and a thorough appreciation of the potential offered by new materials and manufacturing methods.

A marked contrast developed between the parent firm of Edward Gerrard & Sons and T. Gerrard & Co. Ltd. The latter had grown steadily and become increasingly sophisticated and scientifically advanced in its work and the materials used, keeping up with technological advances. Back in Camden Town meanwhile, the original business remained relatively small and relied on ingenuity and living on its collective wits to keep going. As their core business, taxidermy, declined with the demise of big game hunting and field sports generally, the institutional demands of educational and scientific training that underpinned the business of T. Gerrard steadily expanded. By the mid 1960s, when the parent company closed, T. Gerrard & Co was still trading. Later it went into partnership with another supplier and became Gerrard & Haig, based in Sussex. But changing times still caught up with them. Other supply houses progressively eroded their market and there was stiff competition from Phillip Harris and the much bigger companies in America, like Ward's Natural Science and Carolina Biological Supply.

These plaster model brains, each on a turned wooden base, cost 12/6d each in the 1930s. They formed a comparative series, from the primitive lamprey and dogfish, to chimpanzee and dog. They were first sold by Edward Gerrard, then the entire line (including the original moulds, and expertise) was transferred to T.Gerrard & Co. Ltd. They were widely purchased by schools, universities and museums. The models were made in London, following guidelines from standard textbooks and each series was approved by "a recognised authority" before being put on sale. T. Gerrard & Co. became the leading post-war suppliers of such models and educational materials. They also made wax models of anatomical abnormalities.

The final blow was the progressive elimination of anatomical studies from the school syllabus and a reduction in the type of practical work that required any kind of specimens, including microscope slides, in schools, universities and medical schools. Few now need such materials and even fewer can afford to purchase them.

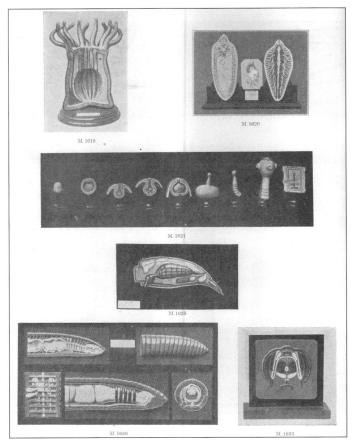

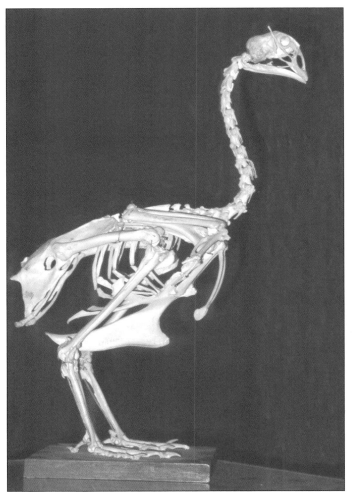

Above: an articulated chicken skeleton by T. Gerrard & Co. Ltd. Most of their osteological preparations bore a prominent white plastic label (right), visible wherever the specimen was displayed. This was a better advertisement than the traditional paper labels hidden from sight beneath the base.

A selection of typical models from T. Gerrard, including both transverse and longitud-inal sections of earthworm and arthropod anatomy, core elements of the curriculum in schools and universities. Being larger and three dimensional, models were easier to see and understand than book illustrations and they were also realistically coloured, which most contemporary textbooks were not.

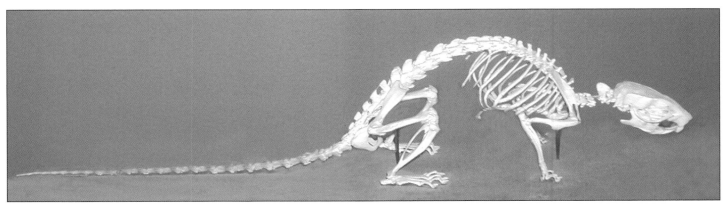

A rat skeleton by T. Gerrard & Co.

Gerrard Hire Ltd.

Chapter 13
Gerrard Hire Ltd.

As part of their attempts to maximise income in the mid 1960's, Gerrards set up a hire division. This offered an opportunity to lend out specimens that would otherwise just be kept in store, mainly things that had been mounted or acquired, but then had not been sold. Often customers did not collect their specimens, particularly dogs, and a significant number of these accumulated. Hiring to photographers, film companies and theatrical productions (and later television) offered the prospect of ongoing income, from renting out spare specimens and unclaimed items. From 1965, this operation was run by Joan Gillett, who had trained in art and sculpture at Sir John Cass College and then spent 20 years in theatre work, making stage props. Her background was thus in stage production and theatrical equipment, so she was an ideal person to manage the hire business.

Initially the hire section operated from a lean-to shed in the Gerrard yard, where it was damp and always very cold. From there, the stock was gradually increased and transferred to a narrow alleyway between two houses in nearby Royal College Street. Here, many of the animals were stored under tarpaulins, but then the alley was roofed in and linked to a large shed like construction (previously a stables) which occupied the garden of an adjacent house in Royal College St. This was later furnished with shelving, floor to ceiling, on which more specimens were stored. The whole place was always dank, musty and cold, even in the height of summer, so a small area was enclosed to create an office that could be kept warm in winter with a single bar electric fire. Here Joan Gillett managed the enterprise as a separate business, Gerrard Hire Ltd (GHL). At first she felt it was spooky to be left alone all day with so many dead animals, but after a while began to treat them almost as familiar friends and family, sharply rebutting any suggestions that her job was an unpleasant one.

For a while, there was a young assistant, also called Joan. Later as the business built up Nellie Lawrence was employed as a full time assistant, formerly one of the furriers working for Gerrards.

When Gerrards went into liquidation in the mid 1960's, the Hire Company was sold to John and Betty Holdcroft to keep it in the family (she being the eldest daughter of Edward Gerrard 4th). GHL received a lot of accumulated bits and pieces from the old firm, including many zoologically interesting items, including mounted huias and similar items, some of which were sold at auction in the 1970's. The hire stock thus comprised many curious

An early Hire Service brochure and later one (right), now referring to the 'Hire Department'

things that were unlikely ever to be hired out, plus a large collection of stuffed rats, cats, game heads and other hirable material. All this was stored in the covered alleyway behind the large wooden gates at 85 Royal College St. From there, specimens were hired out to a constant stream of customers, ranging from film makers to party organizers.

A wicket gate in the large wooden doors opened from Royal College Street into the narrow space between two adjacent houses. Immediately on the left was the office, which contained a desk and a large case of Australian birds topped by a koala that Horace Owen had mounted from a dried skin. Along both sides of the alleyway were stored assorted cats, ranging from a full mount tiger to various domestic pussies, leopards and a couple of lions. The low ceiling supported an area that was reached by climbing a wooden ladder. Here were stored dozens of deer and antelope head mounts, fox masks and a male peacock in full display.

The alley then turned through 90 degrees, to the right was the workroom, the only warm area in the whole place. Here was a small stove, a workbench and space to eat lunch, drink tea or whatever. A selection of tools, paints and other items necessary for repairing hire goods lined the walls. To the left at the end of the alley was a further extension housing shelves from floor to ceiling, arranged in a series of bays. The left wall was hung with game birds 'hanging as dead' and various reptiles and

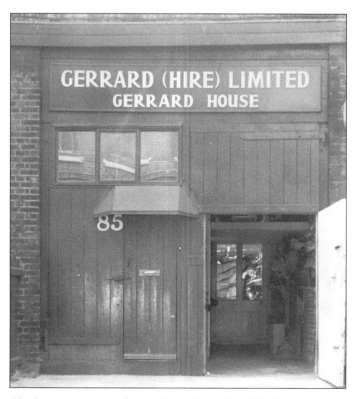

The front entrance to Gerrard Hire Ltd in Royal College Street.

skins. It would have been difficult to fit in any more stock, and exploring what was there took a long time and some acrobatic ability, climbing among the shelves and ladders. Aladdin himself had no better cave than this!

Gerrard Hire Ltd became the leading source of animal material for hire, leading to many bizarre requests. On one occasion, my own visit was interrupted by a telephone call from the Bahamas ordering a goat skull for a fashion photographer's shoot. Despite the substantial insurance valuations and hire charges, customers did not necessarily treat specimens very well. Indeed they were sometimes returned substantially the worse for wear. I saw a blue and yellow macaw that had been liberally touched up with household gloss paint because "it looked a bit faded on screen". A tiger head came back with a hole bored through to allow a pipe to deliver steam as though the animal was smoking, part of a visual joke for television. A bulldog, originally skillfully modelled, became a veteran of many careless hire jobs and began to show signs of wear. It needed new ears, creatively supplied by Joan Gillett using pieces of leather and linoleum. Similarly, "Willy" the lion had been stroked so often that he needed to be fitted with a new mane. In 1966 he appeared at Wembley Stadium, in support of England's World Cup football team.

Cats, large and domestic, were the most popular animals for hire, but also monkeys, parrots and other pets. Stuffed seagulls were also needed, for recreating beach scenes. Vultures were in demand too, and at least one of them was borrowed to be mounted at the end of a hospital bed. Rats were good for business (at up to £10 each per week) as they were in demand for horror movies, always needed in batches, and frequently retained for long periods. However, batches were rarely complete on their return, some having been retained by the hirers or their employees to play practical jokes on others. As a result, there was a constant turnover in the stock of rats, made good by obtaining fresh animals from the Ministry of Agriculture (until they began to charge too much).

Rabbits, pheasants and other animals 'hanging as dead' were also much in demand for filming scenes of hunters returning home, and trophy head mounts were often needed to fit out scenes set in stately homes or haunted castles. The standing tiger was used in advertisements for Esso (until a better one was found) and the full mount polar bear was set up from a dried skin specially for use in promoting a famous brand of Glacier mints. Even the huge bison, nearly 2m tall (6ft) and 3m long went out occasionally, once to a regimental celebration to welcome an American visitor. Items were often sent abroad too, a lion head for an exhibition in Mexico for example and even a kangaroo to Australia.

Some of the animals acquired fame in their own right, particularly those that became familiar to viewers everywhere through their appearance on television. One of these was the upright bear that towered over the set used for filming the 'Steptoe and Son' TV series. Another was the pet ferret that appeared with Compo, a principal character in the long running TV series 'Last of the Summer Wine'. This too normally inhabited Gerrard's shelves, along with the African Grey Parrot that sat on Hughie Green's shoulder when he played Long John Silver for a Christmas TV programme. Large numbers of items were hired for a recreation of the Natural History Museum, needed for the film 'One of our dinosaurs is missing' and an episode of the Hercules Poirot television series included David Suchet as the prissy Belgian detective chasing a villain around in the Natural History Museum. In the background were many of Gerrard's most distinctive creatures, including the baby giraffe, the podgy faced orang utan and the head from a pony that had once been a full mount (none of which appear in the real Natural History Museum of course). Various dogs were hired out to photographers to practice on before attempting to photograph a living animal, so the mounted specimen was never made public. This was not the case when Barclays used a photograph of a stuffed black backed gull in an advertisement. This seemed an odd choice of subject and completely inexplicable given the sad state of the bird, toppling forwards and rather scruffy, but the customer is always right.

The first part of the alleyway (above) was lined with stored cats. Downstairs, the alleyway opened out into a lighter area with a glass roof. Here stood the rogue elephant head, a podgy faced orang utan and a full mount bison. Assorted monkeys were arranged on a shelf, with some glass domes and a baby giraffe standing alongside. A precarious ladder (above) allowed access to the area over the false ceiling, where various skins and mounted heads were kept. Every last bit of wall space was used to support shelves on which animals were stored. (below).

The hire business periodically attracted the attention of would-be purchasers. A flamboyant London animal dealer 'LeBlond's Zoologists' tried to buy the company in 1972, but his offer was declined. Another approach was made by a leading TV hire company in 1990. Maybe there were other approaches too, as the Hire Company was doing good business and was the principal supplier of animals for photographers, film makers and stage and TV productions. In 1978, an approach was made by a 'pet services' company offering "Cremations, home garden burials and taxidermy" who suggested a "mutually rewarding business opportunity" in which they would exhibit a few small stuffed pets in their shop window. This offer was declined.

The fortunes of the hire business fluctuated somewhat. A letter from Joan Gillett written in 1972 said they were "very busy", with long hours being worked, but by 1975 she was describing things as being "very up and down". Nevertheless, the hire company was successful for many years, aided by Horace Owen. He was employed as a part time taxidermist, with a young assistant named Michael Jackson. Horace prepared small specimens (cats, dogs, and other pets, as well as wild birds such as pheasants) brought in by customers who were often glad to have located a taxidermist at all in the days when so few still remained in business. Horace also prepared fresh material for the hire stock and created whole mounts from the many dried cabinet skins left over from the days of the taxidermy company. These included the large tiger and a full mount polar bear.

On the shelves was a vast assortment of skulls, bird and mammal skins, boxes of rats and gerbils, a stuffed seal and a remarkable collection of about 50 full mount dogs. Elephant feet stood about the floor and various plastic bags containing birds in flight hung from the ceiling.

This was the situation when I first visited about 1979. Business was sometimes slack, but it was still hard work. The stock comprised about 10,000 items, much of it very large and difficult to move about. Moreover, the paperwork had also become quite onerous. In the early 1980s many specimens had to be individually registered with the Department of the Environment, as part of the drive to control trade in endangered species. For legal reasons, 'hire' was treated the same as 'sale', so every specimen of a protected species (tigers for example) had to be registered and fitted with an individual identification number, a job that took many days and greatly added to the bookwork associated with the hire business (with no obvious benefit to wildlife conservation). Each specimen of a protected species then had to be booked out on special record forms every time it was hired, then booked back in again, creating a lot of extra paperwork, quite apart from that necessary to administer the hire contracts and keep track of the money paid.

Other changes were also afoot. Filming on location had become much easier for technical reasons, reducing the need to create artificial studio sets. Taxidermy had also become unpopular. Hirings reduced from four or five per day to only a dozen or so per week. Items were often borrowed for only a week (the minimum hire period) not months as had been frequently the case in better times.

By April 1991 it was no longer worth replacing damaged specimens and it also became clear that Joan Gillett would soon retire. The business was not sufficiently buoyant to warrant investing in new stock and employ a successor. It would be sold, en bloc or piecemeal when she went. The logistics of disposal were a daunting prospect to someone (albeit very resourceful) working alone without help. We discussed the situation and it was evident that Joan did not want to simply hand over to one of her competitors, the largest of whom had been arrogantly attempting to crush the hire company financially. A single buyer would pay only so much and this amount would probably still be available if the stock was first filleted of its more interesting and individually saleable items. Auction was risky as there would be a strong possibility of getting left with a lot of unsaleable items, or losing them cheaply, particularly as the taxidermy market had long passed its peak at that time and it was quite difficult to sell things at all.

GHL had no transport and it was important to keep the disposal secret in order to avoid damaging the hire company by advertising its closure. During 1990-1992 I arranged for batches of specimens, including a whole shed full of skulls and horns, to leave London and be deposited with dealers, collectors and educational users. I also arranged for museums to contact GHL direct to obtain particular items, with little noticeable loss to the hire stock. Some of the larger and more interesting hire animals went to Potter's Museum of Curiosities at the Jamaica Inn, Cornwall. These included famous items such as Steptoe's bear. The disposal coincided with the worst period of recession for over half a century and it was not easy to find cash buyers for anything, least of all battered taxidermy.

Many of the worst things were sold on by Cedric Crossfield from his stall in the Portobello Rd, even such bizarre and tasteless items as four zebra legs, rubber 'oven ready', chickens and a cat head with false flesh hanging out of its neck. Some things were exported, some went to buyers with sick tastes and some to respectable homes. I would feel guilty about splitting up the Gerrard stock but it had mostly become very shabby from ill-treatment by generations of hirers. Little was of direct historical or zoological interest, and what was went to appropriate homes to be properly looked after. The hire business closed with the retirement of Joan Gillett, on May the 8th, 1992. I called for the last time a few days before and removed the last unsold item, an awful boar's head. Gerrard Hire Ltd (company no. 00917209) was formally dissolved on October 4th, 1994.

Thus, the remainder of Gerrard's stock was finally dispersed, some of it having been with the family business for more than fifty years. One of the largest single batches of animals had gone to Potter's Museum, which was itself sold by auction in September 2003. By that time, the market for taxidermy curios (even ex-hire company specimens!) had substantially improved and many items were purchased for extraordinary amounts. Among them were Steptoe's bear, which was sold for £6,500, and a baby elephant for £3,700. The baby giraffe that appeared in many old photographs and the Poirot TV film was sold too (for £3,300) and even 'Willy' the full mount lion, complete with his replacement mane, fetched an amazing £1,800.

A hire brochure from the 1970s

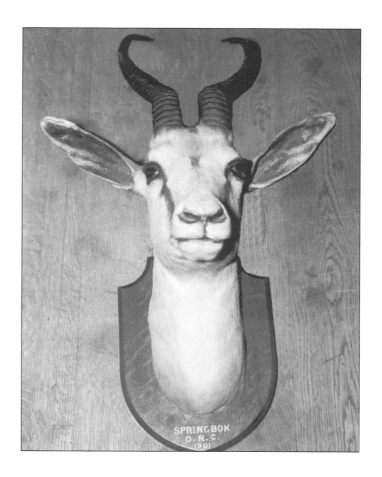

This bear featured in many episodes of the TV series 'Steptoe and Son.'

Right: Trophy heads were often needed to furnish stage and film scenes set in stately homes or ancient castles. They were then frequently borrowed in large batches, often for months at a time, which was good for the hire business.

Joan Gillett in the workroom/ tearoom in 1991. This was the only warm area in the entire place and it tended to serve as the office as well during cold weather.

Gerrard Hire Ltd could supply a choice of lion heads, an ornamental firescreen full of tropical birds, a baby zebra, and all manner of other things, just from the stock inside the front door.

References

Davie, O. (1894)
Methods in the Art of Taxidermy
McKay, Philadelphia

Dollman, J.G. & Burlace, J.B. (1928)
Rowland Ward's Records of Big Game. Rowland
Ward Ltd, London

Edwards, J. (1996)
London Zoo from old photographs, 1852-1914.
The Author, London.

Hillaby, J. (1950)
The House of Gerrard. *Discovery*, 332-334

Mainwaring, H.G. (1920)
A Soldier's Shikar Trips. Grant Richards, London

Morris, P. (2003)
Rowland Ward, Taxidermist to the World.
MPM, Ascot

Moyer, J.W. (1957)
Practical Taxidermy. Thames & Hudson, London

Priestly, H. (1979)
What it cost the day before yesterday. The Museum,
Havant

Rasmusen, C. (2001)
A museum for the people. Scribe Publications,
Melbourne.

Snell, S. & Tucker, P. (2003)
Life Through a Lens. Natural History Museum,
London

Stearn, W.T. (1981)
The Natural History Museum at South Kensington.
Heinemann, London

Appendix- Label Types

Over many years, Gerrards used a wide variety of label designs. Since some of these were applied to trophy heads and other specimens that also bore dated labels, it has sometimes been possible to assign dates to various styles of label. This has been done here. Further dates can be added as more specimens are found, and space has been left to allow for this to be done. In turn, the dates for different label designs may allow a rough estimate of the age of undated specimens to be made. This has now become important when trying to determine whether or not something was killed before 1947, the cut-off date for 'antique' taxidermy. Specimens of protected species that were prepared prior to 1947 can be sold without a licence and are exempt from CITES, which regulates the import and export of animal specimens.

With 'old style' typeface
(and the 'E' of 'Edward' curved like a 'C')

Label type- 1
Description: printed in black
Dates known to have been used:
1897, 1903

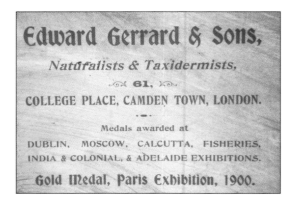

Label type- 2
Description: printed in brown
Dates known to have been used: early 1900s

Label type- 3
Description: printed in brown
Dates known to have been used:
1901, 1908, 1909

The deer head label

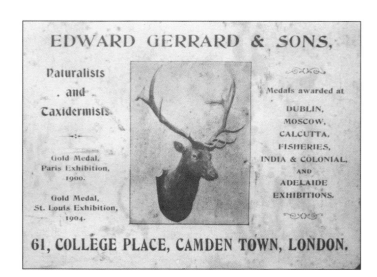

Label type- 4
Description: printed in brown
Dates known to have been used:
1907, 1908, 1909, 1910, 1914, 1921

Labels with different border styles (usually on white paper)

Label type- 5
Description: no '& Sons'
Dates known to have been used:
probably quite early

Label type- 10
Description: also on orange paper
Dates known to have been used:
1924, 1926,1929

Label type- 6
Description:
Dates known to have been used:
after 1900

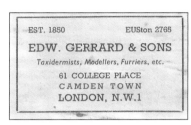

Label type- 11
Description:
Dates known to have been used:
1952, 1956, 1958,1959, 1960

Label type- 7
Description:
Dates known to have been used:
after 1915, 1922, 1932

Label type- 12
Description:
Dates known to have been used:

Label type- 8
Description: also on orange paper
Dates known to have been used:
1924

Label type- 13
Description:
Dates known to have been used:

Label type- 9
Description:
Dates known to have been used:
1924,1927,1931,1939

Label type- 14
Description: narrow rectangle
Dates known to have been used:

Label type- 15
Description: narrow rectangle
Dates known to have been used:

Some more paper labels

(narrow strips without borders)

Label type- 16
Description:
Dates known to have been used:

Label type- 17
Description:
Dates known to have been used:

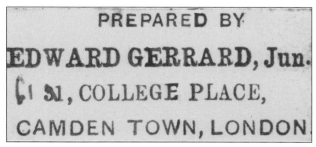

Label type- 18
Description:
Dates known to have been used:

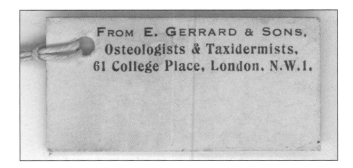

Label type- 19
Description: address misprinted as 51, not 61 College Place
Dates known to have been used:
before 1928

Some paper tie-on labels

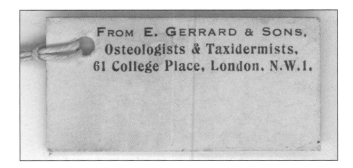

Label type- Tie-on 1
Description: used on skulls, bird and mammal skins
Dates known to have been used:

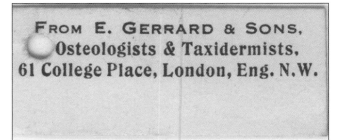

Label type- Tie-on 2
Description: used on skulls, bird and mammal skins
Dates known to have been used:

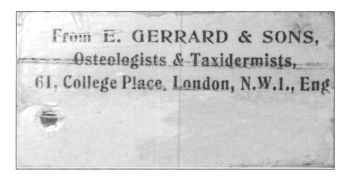

Label type- Tie-on 3
Description: tied or pasted on
Dates known to have been used:

Embroidered fabric labels

Label type- Fabric 1
Description: used on rugs
Dates known to have been used:

Label type- Fabric 2
Description: used on rugs
Dates known to have been used:

Label type- Fabric 3
Description: used on rugs
Dates known to have been used:

Label type- Fabric 4
Description: used on rugs
Dates known to have been used:

Two 'Ivorine' (white plastic labels)

Label type- Ivorine round
Description: about 20mm
diameter, nailed to the
groundwork

**Dates known to have been
used:**
only on very old specimens

Label type- ivorine rectangle
Description: about 40mm long, fixed to wooden bases of
taxidermy and articulated skeletons by pins
Dates known to have been used: probably pre 1940

The rubber stamp (and see title page)

Telephone numbers

The telephone number given in trade directories
changed, but it is not clear exactly when. As a guide,

NORth 2358 was used before World War 2, until
about 1939

EUSton 2765 was used later, at least 1939-1960

Rowland Ward - taxidermist to the world
by P.A. Morris

Rowland Ward died in 1912, but his name lived on, synonymous with high quality and big game taxidermy. The products of Rowland Ward Ltd. are familiar to museums, collectors and big game hunters throughout the world, but seeking details of Ward himself, or the leading firm that he established, is often frustrating and fruitless. Yet it is increasingly recognised that taxidermy and the scientific preservation of animals form an important part of the history of natural history, inviting curiosity about one of the most famous contributors in this area. This book attempts for the first time to put on record the work of Rowland Ward as a tribute to him and to those who worked for the Company that he founded.

'Rowland Ward, taxidermist to the world' comprises 160 A4 pages bound in a blue cloth cover with gold lettering. Nine chapters describe the man himself and his early days in business, the taxidermy workshops during the 20th century and the principal personalities that worked there. Separate chapters cover big game whole mounts, head mounts and birds, with sections on fish taxidermy and 'Wardian' animal furniture. There is also a collation of the many different label types used by Rowland Ward Ltd. for their products. The text, of 55,000 words, is based on more than 20 years research, interviews with former employees and much unpublished material. Over 250 illustrations include line drawings monochrome photographs and copies of old documents.

Copies are available, price £50 (plus £5 p&p) from:

MPM Publishing, West Mains, London Road, Ascot, SL5 7DG